ALASKAN SHIPPING, 1867~1878

ARRIVALS and DEPARTURES at the PORT of SITKA

BY

RICHARD A. PIERCE

THE LIMESTONE PRESS
P. O. Box 1604
Kingston, Ontario

Victoria, B.C. about 1862.

Sitka in 1860, near the close of the
Russian Administration

Steamship *"Gussie Telfair"*.

U.S. Revenue Cutter *"Thomas Corwin"*.

INTRODUCTION

SHIPS PLAY a vital role in the early history of Alaska. Disco-
verers, from Russia and other nations, were borne on ships. Through-
out the Russian era, and later for some years under American rule,
ships were the sole link with the outside world. They brought news,
personnel and supplies, and took away word of local developments,
departing personnel, and the skins, salt fish and other products of
the region. Ship arrivals and sailings are therefore a key to events
and can aid the historian.

This work is based on a list, in manuscript, kept by collectors
of customs at Sitka and now in the U.S. National Archives in Washington, D.C. I have supplemented the original list with the names of a
few vessels which were somehow missed, and with information drawn
from contemporary newspapers, diaries, and other sources. It is a
stark record, but provides a framework from which deductions can be
drawn, and to which other facts may be appended.

Although the original list begins with arrival of the Russian
brig SHELEKHOV, from Victoria, B.C., on 24 October 1867, I have added
data which will illustrate the routine of the Russian period, from
January. Cargoes of ice from Kodiak to San Francisco; salt fish to
Honolulu in exchange for salt; salt fish and seal fat to San Francisco for funds enabling the purchase of supplies in San Francisco and
Victoria--these voyages indicate a thriving, if modest establishment,
and trade patterns worked out over several decades. Only the usual
spring voyages to carry supplies to outlying posts and pick up furs
for delivery to Aian, in eastern Siberia, or to San Francisco, for
trans-shipment to London, are absent, for in April, 1867, news arrived of the treaty of 30 March, providing for sale of Russian America
to the United States. Prince D.M. Maksutov, the last Russian gover-
nor, began to close down company operations. He ceased even to re-
quire formal entry and clearance of vessels in the port of Sitka, on
the ground that it was no longer in his jurisdiction. The U.S. Revenue Cutter LINCOLN arrived to inspect the territory. Hopeful petty
entrepreneurs from Victoria and San Francisco staked out lots as if
in a new gold field, and erected tents for the sale of liquor and
merchandise. In October, naval and chartered cargo vessels began to
appear, and on 18 October the transfer took place.

The orderly, paternal, if somewhat archaic practices of the
Russian-American Company were then replaced by a purely military
occupation whose commander's limited authority made him unable to
assume the responsibilities of his Russian predecessor. The natives,
unaccustomed to thinking for themselves, and totally unprepared for
the change, were exploited and debauched. Most of the Russian population were out of work, some had their homes expropriated, and
decent citizens feared molestation by carousing soldiers or riff-raff.
Those who had been inclined to stay on under the new regime sought
transportation home. On 14 December 1867 the ship TSARITSA sailed
for Russia with 168 passengers; on 22 January the bark CYANE carried
69 soldiers of the Russian garrison to eastern Siberia; and on 30
November 1868, 300 more of the Russian population left on the ship
WINGED ARROW.

The liquidation of Russian-American Company property began
before the transfer, and accelerated thereafter. The company's ships
were sold first, redocumented as American vessels. Nature even took
a hand in the transition, wreaking major damage in the heaviest gale
ever known in those parts. Early in 1868, a bulk sale of all remain-
ing trade goods, supplies and furs took place. Ships sailed for
Portland and San Francisco with the accumulated stocks of years--tons
of sheathing metal, sheet lead, cordage, hoop and bar iron, bells,
brass cannon, anchors, linen, calico, and bales of furs from the company warehouses. From the Pribilovs came cargoes of seal skins and
oil. Unrestricted hunting reduced the fur seals so quickly that the
United States government gave Hutchinson, Kohl & Company and its suc-
cessor the Alaska Commercial Company a monopoly and placed quotas
over the annual fur harvest.

Intoxicating liquors were banned under United States statutes
relating to "Indian country," but no adequate provision was made for
enforcement of the law. In the southern archipelago a flock of
schooners flitted among the passages engaged in contraband trade.
The LOUISA C. DOWNES, the NOR'WESTER, the GENERAL HARNEY, the SWEEP-
STAKES and the PIONEER acquired local fame or notoriety, depending on
the point of view. From nearby British territory were smuggled large
quantities of liquor and other goods. The collectors at Sitka com-
plained to superiors that the Hudson's Bay Company steamship OTTER
traded constantly in the islands without reporting. A villainous con-
coction called "hooch," distilled locally, added to the demoralizing
trade in spirits.

In the north, other schooners supplied liquor to the Eskimos, so
disrupting the native way of life that some villages were later wiped
out by starvation. The cutters of the U.S. Revenue Service tried to
curb this traffic, but were too few and usually too slow to catch
more than a few of the culprits. The smugglers boasted openly of their

exploits. Many vessels which called at Sitka cited false destinations. Others never went near Sitka at all; leaving San Francisco for Honolulu, they would there load up with cheap liquor of Hawaiian or European manufacture, clear early in the season, and head north. In Bering Strait they would trade with natives on both the Siberian and Alaskan shores, ever ready to cross over to the unpatrolled Siberian side if a revenue cutter appeared.

During the brief period of prosperity between September 1867 and August 1869, many vessels called at Sitka, but from that time forward the shipping of the port declined sharply. The monthly mail steamer became almost the only means of communication between Sitka and Washington Territory, and all intercourse between Sitka and the western portion of Alaska ceased. The one-time Russian capital had become a backwater. The list carries the story a few months past the departure of the Army on the steamer CALIFORNIA on 17 June 1877. Only on 1 October 1884, when a territorial government was formed, did a revival begin.

Certain personalities, well known in their day, are prominent in the present list. Frequent visitors were the skippers Thomas J. Ainsley, M. C. Erskine, George W. Holden, and John R. Sands. The U.S. Revenue Service captains Bailey, White, Henriques, and Selden appear from time to time. The veteran contraband trader in the Bering Sea area, Captain Henry Ravens, brought the schooner LOUISA C. SIMPSON into Sitka in 1870 and the schooner URANIA in 1872. Vincent Baranowicz, of similar talents, established for years at Kasaan Bay, in the southern archipelago, appears once in his sailing vessel the PIONEER.

Captain Joshua Slocum, famed a generation later as the first man to sail alone around the world, on 10 August 1870 brought the bark CONSTITUTION to Sitka "from Carman Island, Mexico," a voyage overlooked by his biographers. The CONSTITUTION, under another master, called again in the following June, but meanwhile Slocum, in voyages typical of the times, but even more so of the man, took the bark WZSHINGTON from San Francisco to Sydney, married there, and then took bride and bark directly to Cook Inlet, Alaska, to catch and salt a cargo of fish. The vessel was blown ashore at Kasilof and lost, but Slocum and his men built a large whaleboat from her timbers, went on fishing, and acquired a cargo which was taken to market by hired craft.

Certain vessels also stand out--the steamships FIDELITER, the CALIFORNIA, the ill-fated GEORGE S. WRIGHT, and the GUSSIE TELFAIR. Durable reminders of the Russian era were the steamers ALEXANDER and CONSTANTINE, the ROSE (formerly the BARANOV) and the POLITOFSKY; the ship TSESAREVICH, the bark MENSHIKOV and the brig SHELEKHOV.

Additional details may be found in the <u>Daily British Colonist</u>, of Victoria, the <u>Alta California</u>, of San Francisco, and other coast newspapers. Lewis & Dryden's <u>Marine History of the Pacific Northwest</u> contains many facts and rare photographs, although being oriented toward regions farther south, even this useful volume does not provide adequate coverage of Alaska.

Dates in the months prior to September 1867 are in both the old style, twelve days behind, used by the Russians, and the new style. Some of the spelling and wording of the original list has been retained, but some has been altered for the sake of brevity and uniformity. The illustrations are from the Lewis & Dryden volume and contemporary sources.

Richard A. Pierce

Queen's University,

Kingston, Canada.

ARRIVALS and DEPARTURES
at the
PORT of SITKA
1867-1878

<u>1867</u>

18/30 Jan.   Brig CONSTANTINE (Den'gin), from Honolulu with cargo of
             salt and tea.

19/31 Jan.   Brig SHELEKHOV (Hanson), from Honolulu with cargo of salt.

24 Feb./8 Mar.   Steamer CONSTANTINE (Lindfors), from Victoria with
             new boiler and cargo of coal from Nanaimo.

10/22 Mar.   British (Hudson's Bay Company) steamer OTTER, from
             Victoria.

27 Mar./8 Apr.   Bark MENSHIKOV (Kashevarov), from Kodiak with furs.

14/26 Apr.   Steamer ALEXANDER (Boucht), from Victoria with new
             boiler.

24 May/6 June   Br. steamer FIDELITER (Erskine), from Victoria with
             twelve passengers, who erected places of
             business.

? June   Br. steamer OTTER, from Victoria.

ca. 3/15 June   H.M.S. SPARROWHAWK (Cooper), from Victoria with Gover-
             nor Seymour, to settle up H.B.C. affairs in
             Russian America.

3/15 June   American bark DELAWARE (Shillaber), from S.F.

? July   Br. steamer OTTER, from Victoria.

? July   Br. schooner MAJOR, from Victoria.

? July   Sloop MYSTERY, from Victoria.

? July   Schooner NOR'WESTER, from Port Townsend.

? July   Schooner LOUISA DOWNES, from Victoria.

25 July/6 Aug.   Russian ship TSARITSA (Eusalius), from Kronshtadt.

31 July/12 Aug.   U.S. Revenue Cutter LINCOLN (W.A. Howard), from
             S.F. via Victoria, with coastal survey party under
             George Davidson

13/25 Mar. Br. steamer OTTER, for "Kolosh Straits" (Alexander
                Archipelago).

21 Mar./2 Apr. Bark MENSHIKOV (Kashevarov), for Kodiak.

21 Mar./2 Apr. Ship TSESAREVICH (Lindfors), for Kodiak, to take a
                cargo of ice to San Francisco.

10/22 Apr. Br. steamer OTTER, for Victoria, after trading voyage.

12/24 Apr. Brig SHELEKHOV (Den'gin), for Kodiak, Pribilov Islands,
                S.F., and Honolulu.

20 Apr./2 May Brig CONSTANTINE (Hanson), for Kodiak to catch and
                salt a cargo of cod, thence to S.F.

27 Apr./9 May Steamer ALEXANDER (Lemashevskii), for Kodiak and the
                Aleutian Islands.

8/20 May Bark MENSHIKOV (Kashevarov), to Unalaska, Pribilov Islands
                and Redoubt St. Michael.

? May Bark NAKHIMOV (Boucht), for Aian and DeCastrie Bay, Siberia.

? June Steamer CONSTANTINE (Niebaum), for Kodiak, Pribilov Islands,
                and Unalaska.

ca. 3/15 June Br. steamer OTTER, for Victoria.

7/19 June H.M.S. SPARROWHAWK (Cooper), for Victoria.

23 June/4 July Br. steamer FIDELITER, for Victoria.

6/18 July Br. steamer OTTER, for Chilcarethe (?). U.S. Inspector
                of Customs aboard, to settle H.B.C. business
                with Indians.

ca. 29 July Sloop MYSTERY, for Port Townsend.

8/20 Aug. Schooner NOR'WESTER, for Victoria.

10/22 Aug. U.S.R.C. LINCOLN, for Fort Constantine and Unalaska.

4   <u>Arrivals</u>

? Sept.   Brig CONSTANTINE (Hanson), from S.F.

11 Sept.   U.S. ship JAMESTOWN (King), from S.F., "to be purified by
                cold after a bout with yellow fever."

? Sept.   Br. steamer OTTER, from Victoria.

13 Sept.   U.S.S. RESACA. Also for "purification" after yellow fever
                cases.

20 Sept.   Ship TSESAREVICH (Lindfors), from S.F.

? Sept.   Chartered merchant ship BUENAVISTA, from S.F.

ca. 24 Sept.   Hawaiian bark MAMELUKE, from Nanaimo, with coal.

9 Oct.   Ship JOHN L. STEPHENS (C.C. Dall), from S.F., with Brigadier
                General Jefferson C. Davis and 250 soldiers, and
                various would-be settlers and speculators
                eager to purchase assets of the Russian-American
                Company.

                Russian brig CONSTANTINE sold to Russian-American
                Company employee Gustave Niebaum and associates.

                Russian ship TSESAREVICH sold to Adolph Schmid-
                berg.

18 Oct.   U.S. sloop-of-war OSSIPEE, from S.F., with U.S. commissioner
                Rousseau and Russian commissioner Peshchurov.

                <u>Transfer of Alaska to U.S.A.</u>

19 Oct.   U.S.R.C. LINCOLN, from survey voyage.

? Oct.   Russian steamship POLITOVSKI sold to Hutchinson &
                Hirsch.

? Oct.   Russian ship MENSHIKOV sold to Hutchinson &
                Hirsch.

24 Oct.   Russian brig SHELEKHOV (George Den'gin), from S.F. and
                Victoria, with coal.

26/27 Oct.   Great gale at Sitka. Russian steamer ALEXANDER
                collided with ship JOHN L. STEPHENS. Russian
                brig CONSTANTINE wrecked on Japonski Island.
                Ship TSESAREVICH left high and dry until next
                tide. Brig SHELEKHOV hit a rock. Other vessels
                damaged.

28 Oct.   U.S. Sloop-of-war OSSIPEE returns, damaged by storm.

28 Oct.   Hawaiian bark MAMELUKE returns, damaged by storm.

1 Nov.   Collector's List: Russian ship, Boucht, master, from Kastris
                Bay, Alaska. No cargo; ships' stores.
                (Evidently the bark NAKHIMOV, from DeCastrie Bay,
                Siberia. Vessel sold to H.M. Hutchinson and
                renamed CYANE).

12/24 Aug. Schooner LOUISA DOWNES, for Victoria and Port Townsend.

26 Sept. Schooner LANGLEY left.

 ? Sept. Br. steamer OTTER, for Victoria.

25 Oct. Hawaiian bark MAMELUKE (William Lund), for Esquimault, B.C.

26 Oct. U.S. sloop-of-war OSSIPEE, for Portland.

27 Oct. U.S.R.C. LINCOLN, for Stikine, with survey party, thence
              to Victoria and S.F.

1 Nov. Steamer JOHN L. STEPHENS (C.C. Dall), for Victoria and S.F.

26 Dec.   Br. schooner ALERT (McKay), from Victoria.

27 Dec.   Am. schooner GROWLER (H. Coffin), from Port Townsend and
                    Victoria. H.M. Hutchinson aboard, hastening to
                    Sitka to make final purchase of Russian-American
                    Company goods before other buyers.

<u>1868</u>

 5 Jan.   Br. steamer EMMA (Holmes), from Victoria. Passengers, 2.

18 Jan.   Steamer FIDELITER (M.C. Erskine), from Victoria. Passen-
                    gers, 13, including Kinkaid, Postmaster of
                    Alaska, Hon. Ben Truman, U.S. Postal Agent, and
                    U.S. Army colonels Reece and Dennison.

21 Jan.   Brig OLGA (J.G. Sandman), from S.F.

30 Jan.   Schooner NOR'WESTER (A.T. Whitford), from Port Townsend.
                    Collector's note: "Six weeks from Victoria by
                    Inside Passage," implying question as to
                    activities enroute.

 8 Feb.   Br. steamer OTTER (H.G. Lewis), from Victoria. Passengers,
                    17.

6 Nov.   U.S. Sloop-of-war OSSIPEE, for S.F.

12 Nov.   Ship CESAREWITSCH (A. Schmidberg), for S.F. Domestic cargo.

27 Nov.   Brig CONSTANTINE (John Hanson), for trading voyage, N.W.
                    Coast, Alaska, thence to S.F. (Arrived S.F.
                    2 March 1868, with cargo of sealskins from
                    Pribilov Islands).

28 Nov.   Schooner LANGLEY (John Malowanski), for Victoria.

ca. 1 Dec. Hawaiian bark MAMELUKE (William Lund), for British
                    Columbia.

14 Dec.   Russian ship TSARITSA (Eusalius), "for London, England"
                    (actually Honolulu, Callao, Liverpool, and
                    Kronshtadt). Crew, 31; passengers, 168 (inclu-
                    ding 80 Russian families and most of the offi-
                    cials of the former Russian colony).

24 Dec.   Steamer CONSTANTINE, in ballast, for Victoria. Crew, 27;
                    passengers, 9.

<u>1868</u>
4 Jan.   Br. schooner ALERT (McKay), for Victoria. In ballast.
                    Crew, 4.

9 Jan.   Sloop JABEZ HOWE left for Karluk (not on Collector's List).

10 Jan.   Br. steamer EMMA, for Victoria. In ballast.

10 Jan.   Bark MILAN, for Port Townsend.

18 Jan.   U.S. War Steamer RESACA, for S.F. Passengers included
                    Princess Maksutova, wife of former governor,
                    and family, returning to Russia.

21 Jan.   Schooner GROWLER (Coffin), for Port Townsend.

22 Jan.   Russian bark CYANE (Boucht), "for Novogorod, Asia," (accor-
                    ding to another account, "for the Amoor River").
                    Crew, 22; soldiers, 69 (the last of the former
                    Russian garrison).

24 Jan.   Steamer FIDELITER (Erskine), for Victoria and Portland.
                    Passengers, 17.

27 Jan.   Bark MENSHIKOFF (Kashevarov), for Victoria.

8 Feb.   Bark BUENA VISTA (A.K. Kelton), for Port Townsend.

10 Feb.   Brig OLGA (Sandman), for S.F. Crew, 8; passengers, 5.

10 Mar. Bark MENSHIKOFF (Kashevarov), from Victoria. Passengers, 5.

14 Mar. Br. sloop THORNTON (J.D. Warren).

18 Mar. Br. schooner ALERT (McKay), from Victoria.

23 Mar. Bark PERU (Morgan), from Sandwich Islands. Crew, 32; no
        cargo.

24 Mar. Steamer CALIFORNIA (Mason), from S.F. and Victoria. Crew,
        36; passengers, 19.

30 Mar. Steamer FIDELITER (M.C. Erskine), from Portland and Victor-
        ia.

30 Mar. Schooner LANGLEY, from Victoria.

31 Mar. Br. steamer OTTER (W.G. Lewis), from Victoria.

31 Mar. Ship WINGED ARROW (J.R. Sands), from S.F.

 3 Apr. Brig CONSTANTINE (John Hanson), from S.F. Crew, 10.

 3 Apr. Schooner CALDERA (Holcomb).

10 Apr. Schooner THOMAS WOODWARD (Edgequist), from S.F.

10 Apr. Steamer CONSTANTINE (Lindfors), from Victoria. Crew, 28;
        passengers, 5.

13 Apr. Brig OLGA (Sandman), from S.F. Crew, 9; passengers, 6.

 ? Apr. Br. schooner BLACK DIAMOND (W.C. McCulloch), from Nanaimo.

20 Apr. Ship CESAREWITSCH (David Walker), from S.F.

24 Mar.   Bark PERU (Morgan) cleared "on a whaling and sealing
          voyage."

24 Mar.   Br. schooner ALERT (McKay), for Victoria.

25 Mar.   Steamer CALIFORNIA (Mason), for Victoria and S.F.

30 Mar.   Br. sloop THORNTON (Warren), for Victoria.

1 Apr.   Steamer FIDELITER (Erskine), cleared "on a trading and
          sealing voyage on North West Coast of Alaska."

3 Apr.   Br. steamer OTTER (Lewis), for Victoria with special
          permission to touch at Stikine.

6 Apr.   Schooner CALDERA (Holcomb), "for Petropaulski, Asia."

7 Apr.   Ship WINGED ARROW (J.R. Sands) "for North West coast of
          Alaska."

10 Apr.   Schooner THOMAS WOODWARD (Edgequist), "on a trading voyage
          along the North West Coast of Alaska and thence
          to S.F., Cal."

13 Apr.   Brig OLGA, "for Petro-Paulski, Asiatic Coast, with permis-
          sion to touch but not to trade at the Aleutian
          Islands, Ounga, Belkoffskia, Atchta and Attou."

17 Apr.   Schooner LANGLEY (Cozian), on a trading voyage along the
          coast of Alaska and the adjacent American
          islands.

17 Apr.   Brig CONSTANTINE (Fred Reidell), "on a trading voyage along
          the coast of Alaska and adjacent American
          islands and thence to S.F. or Sitka."

20 Apr.   Br. schooner BLACK DIAMOND (McCulloch), for Nanaimo.

20 Apr.   Ship CESAREWITSCH (Walker), for Kodiak (for a cargo of ice),
          and thence to S.F.

24 Apr.   Steamer ALEXANDER (Lindfors), "cleared for Nicolaeffski Asia
          with special clearance to touch at all the tra-
          ding posts of the Russian-American Company on
          the mainland of Alaska and the adjacent islands
          of the territory, for the purpose of closing the
          business of the Russian-American Company under
          the Treaty of March 30, 1867."

27 Apr. Am. schooner PIONEER (Baranowicz), from Port Townsend and
            Victoria.

4 May Schooner FRANCIS A. STEELE, from S.F.

9 May Br. schooner SWEEPSTAKES (A. Heiffer), from Victoria.

18 May Br. sloop OCEAN QUEEN (William H. Smith) from Victoria.
            Crew, 2; passengers, 6. Emil Teichmann, in
            <u>A Journey to Alaska in the Year 1868</u>, describes
            the difficult voyage, which took a month, in the
            small one-masted sailing vessel, "a flat boat of
            scarcely 20 feet long by 8 feet broad, a so-cal-
            led "Plunger," without any gunwale or elevation
            except for a cabin, half sunk in the deck and
            half raised above it, measuring about 12 feet in
            length, 6 in width and 4 in height, which was in-
            tended to shelter for a voyage of a week's dura-
            tion the six passengers and two seamen as well as
            their luggage, which had to be reduced to a mini-
            mum."

23 May U.S. Revenue steamer WAYANDA (J.W. White).

6 June Schooner LOUISA DOWNS (M. Sullivan), from Port Townsend.

ca. 15 June U.S. steamer SAGINAW, from second visit to site of wreck
            of the schooner GROWLER.

15 June Br. schooner BLACK DIAMOND (McCulloch), from Nanaimo, with
            coal.

24 June Bark DELAWARE (Shillaber), from S.F.

30 Apr. Am. schooner PIONEER (Kashevarov), "for Chasan, Alaska."

 9 May Bark MENSHIKOFF (Kashevarov), "for Ounalaska, St. Georges
             and St. Pauls Islands." Crew, 26.
             <u>Alaska Herald</u>, 20 Nov. 1868, states that early in
             1868 Messrs. A. Wassermann of S.F. sent the
             MENSHIKOFF from S.F. to seek the winter habita-
             tion of fur seals. They failed, but established
             several posts on the Siberian mainland, including
             one at Plover Bay.

23 May Steamer CONSTANTINE (Benzemann), "for the Northwest of Alaska
             and the Aleutian Islands." Crew, 30; passengers,
             17. The latter included Gen. Dana, who debarked
             at Kodiak to examine the ice exporting business,
             and the Russian commissioner Capt. Peshchurov,
             Russian-American Company representative Capt.
             Koskull, and the bishop of the Russian Orthodox
             Church. <u>Daily British Colonist</u>, 22 Apr. 1868,
             states vessel was "to visit Russian fur company
             stations at Amur River before being turned over
             to the American Fur Company."

23 May Brig SHELIKOFF (Daigen?), "for coast of Alaska and Aleutian
             Islands." Crew, 21; passengers, 37.

23 May Br. sloop OCEAN QUEEN (Smith) cleared for Victoria, in bal-
             last. Crew, 2; passengers, 3.

 ? May U.S. Revenue steamer WAYANDA (J.W. White), for the north.

25 May U.S. steamer SAGINAW (Mitchell) left for Stakine and Victoria

30 May U.S. store ship JAMESTOWN, for Esquimault, with discharged
             soldiers and sailors and Quartermaster Depart-
             ment employees, after nine months at Sitka. To
             proceed to Mare Island and be decommissioned.

 4 June Schooner PIONEER (Kashevarov), "for a trading voyage along
             the coast of Alaska and the adjacent American
             islands."

19 June Schooner BLACK DIAMOND (McCulloch), for Victoria and Nanai-
             mo.

20 June Foreign (undocumented) schooner SWEEPSTAKES (Theo. Halten),
             for a trading voyage south of Sitka to Prince of
             Wales Island.

20 June Schooner LOUISA DOWNS (Sullivan), for a trading and pros-
             pecting voyage south and east of Sitka to
             Tarkou and Stikine rivers.

13 July   Steamer GEORGE S. WRIGHT (W. Langdon), from Portland and
              Victoria.

17 July   Ship WINGED ARROW (Sands), from the North West Coast of
              Alaska.

20 July   Steamer CONSTANTINE (Benzemann), from North West Coast of
              Alaska. Crew, 30; passengers, 42.

20 July   Bark MENSHIKOFF (Kashevarov), from North West Coast of
              Alaska. Passengers, 7.

28 July   Bark PERU (Comstock), from Honolulu.

31 July   Russian bark CYANE, from Asiatic coast and Aleutian Islands.

 6 Aug.   Am. schooner SWEEPSTAKES (undocumented) (Haltern), for
              trading voyage along the North West Coast.

12 Aug.   Schooner LANGLEY (Cozian), from a trading voyage along the
              North West Coast.

18 Aug.   Steamship PACIFIC (Winsor), from S.F. & Victoria. Entered
              from Stikine. Carried Gen. Halleck and staff,
              and Muybridge, first to photograph Alaska.

22 Aug.   Br. schooner BLACK DIAMOND (Ferguson), from Nanaimo.

28 Aug.   Steamer ALEXANDER (A. Lindfors), "from the Asiatic coast and
              the Aleutian islands."

31 Aug.   Schooner JOHN BRIGHT (John R. Sands), from S.F.

12 Sept. Br. steamer OTTER (H.G. Lewis), from Victoria.

29 Sept. Schooner ANN ELIZA (J.B. Morrison), from S.F.

29 Sept. Schooner SWEEPSTAKES (undocumented) (Haltern), from a
              trading voyage to Chilcat River, Alaska.

16 July Bark DELAWARE, for S.F. Crew, 11; passengers, 11.

ca. 17 July Steamer GEORGE S. WRIGHT (Langdon), for Victoria.

17 July Ship WINGED ARROW (Sands), for S.F.

24 July Steamer CONSTANTINE (H.M. Hutchinson), for Victoria and S.F.
             Purchased by Hutchinson, Kohl & Co., the vessel
             ran aground off B.C. coast through pilot error.
             Extensive damage; goods removed to Victoria.

31 July Bark PERU (Comstock), "on a whaling and sealing voyage in
             Behring Sea."

 6 Aug. Schooner SWEEPSTAKES, for a trading voyage south and east of
             Sitka to Prince of Wales Island.

21 Aug. Steamship PACIFIC (Winsor), for Victoria. Gen. Halleck,
             and wife and son aboard.

27 Aug. Br. schooner BLACK DIAMOND, for Nanaimo, in ballast.

14 Sept. Schooner NOR'WESTER (Bendel), for a trading voyage east of
             Sitka.

15 Sept. Schooner JOHN BRIGHT (Rink), for S.F.

15 Sept. Br. steamer OTTER, "on a special permit" to the Stikine
             River, George W. Moore, sp. agent.

15 Sept. Steamer ALEXANDER (W.E. Mason), for trading posts of
             Hutchinson, Kohl & Co. on the Aleutian Islands
             and St. Pauls.

26 Sept. Am. bark CYANE (J.R. Sands), for S.F. (Former NAKHIMOV,
             purchased by Hutchinson, Kohl &Co. and renamed.

 2 Oct.   Russian ship WINGED ARROW (Benzemann), from S.F., on a
                special permit. Purchased by Prince Maksutov
                from Hutchinson, Kohl & Co. and sent to Sitka to
                transport remaining Russians.

 5 Oct.   Steamer FIDELITER (Winsor), from Aleutian Islands and St.
                Paul.

18 Oct.   Schooner NOR'WESTER (B. Bendell), from Chilcat.

 4 Nov.   Bark DELAWARE (Robertson), from S.F. and Kodiak. U.S. pay-
                master Col. Dana arrived on her from Kodiak,
                where he had been paying off U.S. troops.

13 Nov.   Steamer ALEXANDER (Erskine), from St. Pauls and Aleutians.

17 Dec.   Br. steamer OTTER, from Victoria.

26 Dec.   Schooner GENERAL HARNEY.

<u>1869</u>

 6 Jan.   U.S. Revenue Steamer WAYANDA (J. White), from S.F. and
                Victoria.

 4 Feb.   Br. steamer OTTER, from Victoria.

15 Feb.   Br. schooner FAVORITE, from Victoria.
18 Feb.   Schooner IDAHO, from S.F.

23 Feb.   Bark MONTICELLO, from Honolulu.

5 Oct.   Schooner ANN ELIZA (Morrison), for a trading voyage along
                 the North West Coast of Alaska and thence to
                 S.F.

10 Oct. Steamer FIDELITER (Winsor), for Victoria.

10 Oct. Schooner LOUISA DOWNES (Hanson), for trading voyage north
                 and east of Sitka.

31 Oct. Schooner LANGLEY (Cozian), for Victoria.

14 Nov. Brig SHELEKHOFF (Curopheff ?), for S.F.

16 Nov. Steamer ALEXANDER (W.C. Erskine), for S.F., with 21 passen-
                 gers.

30 Nov. Russian ship WINGED ARROW (Benzemann), for Kronshtadt,
                 Russia, via Honolulu, St. Catherines and London.
                 <u>Sitka Times</u>, 7 Nov., stated that vessel would
                 take 186 persons, including men, women and
                 children, the last large group of Russians in
                 Alaska to leave for the homeland.

22 Dec. Br. steamer OTTER, for Victoria.

<u>1869</u>

6 Jan.   Bark MENSHIKOFF, for S.F.

13 Jan. U.S.S. SAGINAW, for a cruise northward.

20 Jan. Schooner GENERAL HARNEY, for S.F.

8 Feb.   Br. steamer OTTER, for Victoria.

12 Feb. Brig SHELEKHOFF, for S.F.

19 Feb. Schooner IDAHO, for the Northwest Coast.

25 Feb. Br. schooner FAVORITE.

27 Feb. Bark MONTICELLO, for Northwest Coast of Alaska

Arrivals

4 Mar. Schooner LEGAL TENDER, from S.F.

4 Mar. Steamer GEORGE S. WRIGHT, from Portland, Victoria, and Nanaimo.

16 Mar. (Un-named vessel), from S.F.

16 Mar. Schooner LEWIS PERRY, from S.F.

16 Mar. Bark CYANE (Small), from S.F. and Victoria.

17 Mar. Bark FRANCIS PALMER, from S.F.

22 Mar. Schooner ALICE, from S.F.

23 Mar. Steamer CONSTANTINE, from S.F. Beginning of regular postal service on the Alaska route.

24 Mar. Schooner LUELLA, from S.F.

30 Mar. Schooner GENERAL HARNEY, from S.F.

19 Apr. Bark KUTUSOFF, from Nanaimo.

20 Apr. Bark FRANCIS PALMER, from Kodiak

24 Apr. Schooner LIZZIE SHA.

? Apr. Schooner ALASKA

26 Apr. Brig COMMODORE, from S.F.

26 Apr. Steamer YOUKON, from S.F., brought on deck of brig COMMODORE for further transport to St. Michael.

29 Apr. U.S. Revenue Cutter LINCOLN, from S.F.

8 May. Ship CESAREWITSCH, from S.F.

10 May Brig OLGA.

10 May Schooner FRANCIS L. STEELE, from S.F.

4 Mar. Schooner LEGAL TENDER, for St. George's Island.

10 Mar. Steamer GEORGE S. WRIGHT, for Portland.

16 Mar. U.S.S. SAGINAW.

18 Mar. Bark CYANE left for Northwest Coast of Alaska.

23 Mar. Bark FRANCIS PALMER, for Kodiak.

24 Mar. Schooner LEWIS PERRY, for Northwest Coast.
24 Mar. Steamer CONSTANTINE, for Northwest Coast.
26 Mar. Schooner LUELLA, for Northwest Coast of Alaska.
27 Mar. Schooner ALICE, for Petropavlovsk, Kamchatka.

20 Apr. Bark FRANCIS PALMER, for S.F.
22 Apr. Schooner GENERAL HARNEY.
24 Apr. Schooner LIZZIE SHA

8 May Brig COMMODORE, for north.
8 May Steamer YOUKON, for north. On 4 July 1869, Capt. Charles F.
               Raymond, U.S. Army, embarked on her, taking her
               upriver to Fort Yukon, from which, being on U.S.
               territory, the British retired.

8 May Ship CESAREWITSCH.

12 May Brig OLGA.
14 May Bark KUTUSOFF, for Port Townsend.
14 May Schooner FRANCIS L. STEELE
 ? May U.S. Revenue Cutter LINCOLN (Henriques), to the west.
20 May Schooner NOR'WESTER, for Forts Tongass and Wrangell.

5 June   Schooner SWEEPSTAKES, from Stikine River, undocumented.

30 June Br. steamer EMMA (Peter Holmes), from Victoria, in ballast.

3 July   U.S. transport NEWBERN (Capt. W. Freeman, Jr.).

10 July Steamer MAJOR (John Cook), from the Chilkat country,
               undocumented.

13 July Schooner NOR'WESTER (William Phillips).

22 July Steamer FIDELITER (J.W. White), chartered by U.S. Government
               for tour of Maj. Gen. Thomas, new commander of
               the Pacific Division of the Army.

31 July Schooner SWEEPSTAKES (James Keen), from Chilkat.

31 July Steamer ACTIVE (C.C. Dall). Hon. William H. Seward aboard.

6 Aug.   Schooner LANGLEY (Michael Sullivan), undocumented, "from the
               North."

11 Aug. U.S. Revenue Cutter LINCOLN (Capt. J.A. Henriques), from
               Northwest Coast of Alaska.

21 Aug. Schooner PAGE (N. Holcomb), from trading voyage in district.

21 Aug. Schooner NOR'WESTER (William Phillips), from trading voyage
               in district.

22 Aug. Schooner SWEEPSTAKES (James Keen), from trading voyage in
               district.

25 Aug. U.S. Revenue Cutter LINCOLN (Capt. J.A. Henriques), from
               cruise south.

26 May   Steamer CONSTANTINE, for Victoria and S.F.

ca. 30 May U.S. Revenue Cutter RELIANCE (J.M. Selden), for S.F.

 1 June   Schooner FANNY, for S.F. via Northwest Coast of Alaska.

 4 June   Schooner LANGLEY (Sullivan), for Northwest Coast of Alaska.

15 June   Schooner MAJOR, coastwise in Alaska Territory, undocumented.

24 June   Schooner SWEEPSTAKES, for Cook Inlet and Copper River, for
          trade.

 6 July   Br. steamer EMMA (Peter Holmes), for Victoria.

21 July   Schooner NOR'WESTER (William P. Phillipson), for trading
          voyage in Alaska Territory.

24 July   U.S. transport steamer NEWBERN (Freeman), for S.F.

25 July   Steamer FIDELITER (J.W. White), chartered by the U.S. Gov-
          ernment), for the Northwest Coast of Alaska.
          Gen. Thomas and staff on board.

27 July   Schooner SWEEPSTAKES (James Keen), undocumented, for a
          trading voyage in Alaska Territory.

31 July   Schooner MAJOR (Henry Thin), undocumented, for a trading
          voyage in Alaska Territory.

13 Aug.   S.S. ACTIVE (C.C. Dall), for Victoria and S.F. The Seward
          party aboard.

14 Aug.   U.S. Revenue Cutter LINCOLN (Capt. J.A. Henriques), for
          cruise as far as U.S. Boundary Line, to
          accompany S.S. ACTIVE.

22 Aug.   Schooner PAGE (N. Holcomb), for S.F.

23 Aug.   Schooner NOR'WESTER (William Phillips), for trading voyage
          south in district.

24 Aug.   Schooner SWEEPSTAKES (James Keen), for trading voyage south
          in district.

28 Aug.   Steamship FIDELITER (Capt. John A. White, U.S.R.S.), from
          the west.

8 Sept.   U.S. transport NEWBERN (Capt. Freeman, Jr.), from S.F. via
          Victoria, Tongass and Wrangell.

9 Sept.   Schooner SWEEPSTAKES (James Keen), from Awk.

13 Sept. Schooner, GENERAL HARNEY (Marquis Lindstrom?), from Kodiak
          and Kenai.

16 Sept. U.S. Revenue Cutter LINCOLN, from Tongass.

17 Sept. U.S. Revenue Cutter RELIANCE (Capt. J. M. Selden), from
          S.F.

19 Sept. Schooner LEWIS PERRY (John R. Sands), from Unalaska.

ca. 5 Oct. U.S. Sloop-of-war CYANE (Lt. Comdr. N.M. Dyer).

23 Oct.   U.S. Revenue Cutter LINCOLN (Capt. Evans), from St. Paul.

2 Nov.   Steamer CONSTANTINE (M.C. Erskine), from Port Townsend.
3 Nov.   Schooner MAJOR (Henry Thin).
5 Nov.   Schooner SWEEPSTAKES (James W. Keene).

6 Nov.   Schooner NOR'WESTER (Phillips).

29 Nov. Steamer CONSTANTINE (M.C. Erskine).

20 Dec. Steamer NEWBERN (Capt. W. Freeman, Jr.), from S.F.

<u>1870</u>

4 Jan.   Brig OLGA (John G. Sandman), from Fort Kenai.

26 Jan. Schooner GENERAL HARNEY (Thomas K. Lee), from S.F.

31 Aug.   Steamship FIDELITER (Capt. White), for S.F.

3 Sept.   U.S. Revenue Cutter LINCOLN (Capt. J.A. Henriques), for
          cruise south, as far as Awk.

11 Sept. U.S. Revenue Cutter LINCOLN (Capt. David Evans), for
          Tongass.

18 Sept. Schooner GENERAL HARNEY (T.K. Lee), for Northwest Coast.

18 Sept. Schooner GENERAL HARNEY (T.K. Lee), for Northwest Coast.

18 Sept. U.S. Transport steamer NEWBERN (Capt. James Freeman, Jr.),
          for Northwest Coast with Army supplies.

22 Sept. U.S. Revenue Cutter LINCOLN (Capt. David Evans), for
          Northwest Coast.

25 Sept. Schooner LEWIS PERRY (J.R. Sands), for S.F.

15 Oct.   Schooner LANGLEY (Michael Sullivan), for trading voyage in
          the district.

16 Oct.   Schooner SWEEPSTAKES (James W. Keene), for a trading voyage
          in the district.

26 Oct.   U.S. Transport NEWBERN (Capt. Freeman), for S.F.

? Oct.   Steamer CONSTANTINE (M.C. Erskine), for Nanaimo and Port
          Townsend.

1 Dec.   U.S. Revenue Cutter LINCOLN (Capt. David Evans), for S.F.

5 Dec.   U.S. Mail Steamer CONSTANTINE (M.C. Erskine), for Port
          Townsend.

13 Dec.   Schooner SWEEPSTAKES (William Philips), for trading voyage
          in the District of Alaska.

<u>1870</u>

8 Jan.   Steamer CONSTANTINE (M.C. Erskine), for Port Townsend.

10 Jan.   Steamer NEWBERN (W. Freeman, Jr.), for S.F.

15 Jan.   Brig OLGA (John G. Sandman), for S.F.

27 Jan. Steamer CONSTANTINE (M.C. Erskine), from Port Townsend and
         Nanaimo.

12 Feb. Schooner MAJOR (James Strachan), from trading voyage.

28 Feb. Steamer CONSTANTINE (W.C. Erskine), from Port Townsend via
         Nanaimo.

 4 Mar. Schooner MAJOR (James Strachan), from trading voyage.

 9 Mar. Schooner SWEEPSTAKES (William Phillips), from trading
         voyage.

25 Mar. Brig OLGA (John G. Sandman), from S.F.

25 Mar. Bark ROBERT PORTER (Robert Killman), from S.F.

31 Mar. Steamer CONSTANTINE (D.K. Small), from Port Townsend.

15 Apr. Brig L.P. FOSTER (James Mills), from S.F.

28 Apr. Steamer CONSTANTINE (D.K. Small), from Port Townsend via
         Nanaimo.

12 May   U.S. Steamer NEWBERN (William Freeman, Jr.), from S.F.

18 May   Schooner GENERAL HARNEY (Thomas K. Lee), from a trading
         cruise in the District.

23 May   Schooner SWEEPSTAKES (William Phillips), from trading voyage
         in the District.

31 May   Steamer CONSTANTINE (D.K. Small), from Port Townsend, W.T.

10 June Steamer CONSTANTINE (D.K. Small), from New Chuck, A.T.

13 June Schooner FLYING MIST (W.S. Sadler), from S.F.

 4 Feb.   Steamer CONSTANTINE (M.C. Erskine), for Naimo   and Port
          Townsend.

 7 Feb.   Schooner MAJOR (James Strachan), for trading voyage in the
          District of Alaska.

10 Feb.   Schooner GENERAL HARNEY (Thomas H. Lee), from trading voyage
          in the District of Alaska.

28 Mar.   Brig OLGA (John G. Sandman), for Kodiak and Petropavlovsk,
          Russian possessions.

 2 Apr.   Steamer CONSTANTINE (D.K. Small), for Port Townsend via
          Nanaimo.

 3 Apr.   Steamer CONSTANTINE (M.C. Erskine), for Port Townsend via
          Nanaimo.

29 Apr.   Bark ROBERT PORTER (Robert Killman), to Port Townsend.

 3 May   Brig L.P. FOSTER (James Mills), for Unalaska.

 4 May   Steamer CONSTANTINE (D.K. Small), for Port Townsend via
          Nanaimo.

 7 May   U.S. Revenue Cutter RELIANCE (Capt. J.M. Selden), for Port
          Townsend.
12 May   Schooner EDWIN H. FRANCIS (Makar Ignatieff), for trading
          voyage in the District of Alaska.

21 May   Schooner NOR'WESTER (John Cook), for trading voyage in the
          District of Alaska.

23 May   Schooner GENERAL HARNEY (Thomas K. Lee), for trading voyage
          in the District of Alaska.

24 May   U.S. Steamer NEWBERN (Capt. W. Freeman, Jr.), for cruise to
          the westward, via Kodiac, Ounalaska, St. Paul,
          etc.

 1 June   Steamer CONSTANTINE (D.K. Small), for New Chuck, A.T.

14 June   Schooner FLYING MIST (W.S. Sadler), for S.F. via fishing
          cruise.

15 June   Steamer CONSTANTINE (D.K. Small), for Port Townsend.

28 June   U.S. Steamer NEWBERN (W. Freeman, Jr.), from cruise to the
              westward.

 7 July   U.S. Steamer NEWBERN (Capt. W. Freeman, Jr.), from Chilcat.

 8 July   Schooner NOR'WESTER (John Cook), from trading voyage.

 9 July   Steamer CONSTANTINE (D.K. Small), from Port Townsend via
              Nanaimo.

13 July   Schooner PIONEER (Vincent Baronovich), from Kodiak.

15 July   Schooner EDWIN H. FRANCIS (Macar Ignatiff), from trading
              voyage.

26 July   Schooner SWEEPSTAKES (William Phillips), from Hamilton
              Fishery.

27 July   Steamer GEORGE S. WRIGHT (N.L. Rogers), from Astoria, Oregon,
              via Nanaimo.

 9 Aug.   Schooner PETALUMA (J.H. Hewitt), from Kodiak.

10 Aug.   Bark CONSTITUTION (Joshua Slocum), from Carman Island,
              Mexico.

13 Aug.   Schooner MAJOR (James Walker), from trading voyage.

16 Aug.   Arrived under seizure, schooner LOUISA C. SIMPSON (Henry
              Ravens), from Kotzebue Sound, Arctic Ocean,
              by Revenue Cutter LINCOLN.

22 Aug.   Schooner EDWIN H. FRANCIS (Macar Ignatiff), from trading
              voyage in the District.

23 Aug.   Steamer GEORGE S. WRIGHT (F.C. Waitt), from Portland.

30 Aug.   U.S. Revenue Cutter RELIANCE (J.M. Selden), from cruise to
              the Arctic Ocean and Behring Sea.

30 Aug.   Schooner LOUISA SIMPSON (H. Ravens), in company with RELIANCE
              having fell in with her some 20 miles out to sea
              and returned to obtain further testimony in

21 June   Schooner SWEEPSTAKES (William Phillips), for Hamilton
               Fishery, A.T.

? July   Steamer NEWBERN (W. Freeman, Jr.), for Chilcat River, via
               Hutchenu.

12 July   U.S.Q.M. Steamer NEWBERN (W. Freeman), for S.F. via Vic-
               toria.

14 July   Schooner MAJOR (James Walker), for trading voyage in the
               District.

14 July   Schooner PIONEER (Vincent Baronovich), for Kassan, A.T.

15 July   Steamer CONSTANTINE (D.K. Small), for Port Townsend, via
               Nanaimo.

16 July   Schooner EDWIN H. FRANCIS (Micah Ignatiff), for trading
               voyage in the District.

18 July   Schooner NOR'WESTER (John Cook), for prospecting tour in
               the District.

29 July   Steamer GEORGE S. WRIGHT (N.L. Rogers), for Portland, via
               Nanaimo.

6 Aug.   Schooner SWEEPSTAKES (William Phillips), on trading voyage
               to Chilcat and Tacoo.

11 Aug.   Schooner PETALUMA (James H. Hewitt), for Kodiak.

26 Aug.   Steamer GEORGE S. WRIGHT (F.C. Waitt), for Portland, via
               Nanaimo.

27 Aug.   Schooner LOUISA SIMPSON (Henry Ravens), for Portland, under
               seizure, in charge of Lieut. Thomas Mason,
               U.S.R.C. RELIANCE.

in relation to the SIMPSON's violations of the
Revenue Laws.

30 Aug.   Schooner SHOOTING STAR (J.P. Stimpson), from Kodiak.

31 Aug.   Steamer NEWBERN (W. Freeman), from S.F.

 2 Sept. Schooner CALIFORNIA (Alfred Metcalf), from S.F.

 2 Sept. Schooner FLYING MIST (   ), from S.F.

 2 Sept. Schooner NOR'WESTER (John Cook), from Tacoo.

12 Sept. Schooner SWEEPSTAKES (Billy Phillips), from trading voyage
             from Chilcat.

22 Sept. Steamer NEWBERN (W. Freeman, Jr.), from Kodiak and Kenay.

24 Sept. Schooner GENERAL HARNEY (Thomas H. Lee), from Ounalaska.

27 Sept. Steamer GEORGE S. WRIGHT (F.C. Waite), from Portland via
             Nanaimo.

28 Sept. U.S. Steamer NEWBERN (W. Freeman), from Wrangel with troops.

 4 Oct.   U.S. Schooner MARGARET (Harris), from Kodiak.

24 Oct.   Brig OLGA (John G. Sandman), from Comadore Islands via
             Kodiak.

27 Oct.   Steamer GEORGE S. WRIGHT (F.C. Waite), from Portland.

25 Nov.   Schooner EDWIN H. FRANCIS (Doyle), from trading voyage in the
             District.

29 Nov.   Steamer NEWBERN (W. Freeman, Jr.), from S.F.

 1 Dec.   Steamer CALIFORNIA (N.L. Rogers), from Portland via Victoria
             and Nanaimo.

 5 Dec.   Captain John Cook, master of the schooner NOR'WESTER, arrived
             in Port with his crew, in a small boat, his ves-
             sel having blown on the Rocks in Clarence Straits.

2 Sept.   Schooner LOUISA SIMPSON (H. Ravens), for Portland.

5 Sept.   Steamer NEWBERN (W. Freeman, Jr.), for Kodiak and Kenay.

6 Sept.   Schooner FLYING MIST (Warenden?), for S.F. via Hamilton
               Fisheries.

7 Sept.   Steamer SHOOTING STAR (F.T. Stimson), for S.F. via Vishing
               Banks.

8 Sept.   Schooner CALIFORNIA (Alfred Metcalf), for Port Townsend.

12 Sept.   Schooner EDWIN H. FRANCIS (Edward Doyle), for trading
               voyage in the District.

24 Sept.   Steamer NEWBERN (W. Freeman, Jr.), for Wrangel, A.T.

30 Sept.   Steamer GEORGE S. WRIGHT (F.C. Waite), for Portland via
               Nanaimo.

1 Oct.   Schooner GENERAL HARNEY (T.K. Lee), for S.F.

3 Oct.   Steamer NEWBERN (W. Freeman Jr.), for Tongas, Nanaimo, and
               S.F.

5 Oct.   Schooner SWEEPSTAKES (William Phillips), for Clawok and
               Fort Tongass.

6 Oct.   Schooner NOR'WESTER (John Cook), for Wrangel, A.T.   (See
               Arrivals, 5 December).

26 Oct.   Brig OLGA (John G. Sandman), for Kodiak.

29 Oct.   Steamer GEORGE S. WRIGHT (F.C. Waite), for Wrangel, Tongass,
               Nanaimo, San Juan, Astoria, and Portland.

3 Dec.   Steamer CALIFORNIA (Nat. L. Rogers), for Nanaimo, Victoria
               and Portland.

5 Dec.   Steamer NEWBERN (W. Freeman, Jr.), for S.F.

15 Dec. Schooner SWEEPSTAKES (William Phillips), from trading
                  voyage in the District.

15 Dec. U.S.S. Ship SARANAC (James H. Spotts), from S.F.

31 Dec. Schooner MARY TAYLOR (John Waller), from S.F.

<u>1871</u>

 9 Jan. Steamer GEORGE S. WRIGHT (Nat. L. Rogers), from Portland.

10 Feb. Steamer GEORGE S. WRIGHT (Nat. L. Rogers), from Portland.

 2 Mar. Schooner SWEEPSTAKES (George Dickinson) put back in dis-
                  tress from voyage to Hamiltons Fisheries.

 5 Mar. Canoe, containing 3 Indians Edw. Doyle, Michel Batten &
                  Griffin.

 6 Mar. Schooner CLARA L. WEST (Henry Corkoran), from Kodiak.

20 Mar. Steamer CALIFORNIA (John Hayes), from Portland.

31 Mar. Schooner SWEEPSTAKES (William Phillips) returned, in
                  distress, from voyage to Hamiltons fisheries.

 8 Apr. Ship CEZAROWITCH (John A. May), 17 days from S.F.

15 Apr. Steamer GEORGE S. WRIGHT (Nat. L. Rogers), from Portland and
                  Nanaimo.

 3 May   Schooner MARY TAYLOR (John Waller), from S.F.

 8 May   Steamer GEORGE S. WRIGHT (Nat. L. Rogers), from Portland and
                  Nanaimo.

23 May   Schooner URANIA (Henry Ravens), from S.F.

23 May   U.S. Revenue Cutter LINCOLN (Lieut. Hooper), from Port Town-
                  send on a cruise.

24 May   Schooner SWEEPSTAKES (William Phillipson), from Hamilton
                  Fishery.

22 Dec. U.S. Ship CYANE (Alfred Hopkins), for Tehuantepec, Mexico.

22 Dec. U.S.S. Ship SARANAC (James H. Spotts), for Port Townsend,
          Victoria, and S.F.

<u>1871</u>

7 Jan. Schooner MARY TAYLOR (John Waller), for S.F.

11 Jan. Steamer GEORGE S. WRIGHT (Nat. L. Rogers), for Portland and
          Nanaimo.

11 Jan. U.S. Revenue Cutter RELIANCE (Lieut. William C. Piggott),
          for Port Townsend.

13 Feb. Steamer GEORGE S. WRIGHT (Nat. L. Rogers), for Portland.

15 Feb. Schooner SWEEPSTAKES (George Dickinson), for Hamilton
          Fisheries.

23 Mar. Steamer CALIFORNIA (John Hayes), for Portland.

23 Mar. Schooner CLARA L. WEST (Thicken Ivanoff), for Kodiak.

23 Mar. Schooner SWEEPSTAKES (William Phillips), for Hamilton
          fishery.

17 Apr. Ship CEZAROWITCH (John A. May), for Kodiak.

17 Apr. Steamer GEORGE S. WRIGHT (Nat. L. Rogers), for Portland.

8 May Steamer GEORGE S. WRIGHT (Nat. L. Rogers), for Nanaimo and
          Portland.

13 May Schooner MARY TAYLOR (John Waller), for S.F., under seizure
          in charge of P. Corcoran, Inspector, as Prize-
          master

26 May Schooner URANIA (Henry Ravens), for S.F. via trading voyage
          in the waters of Alaska.

 2 June   Steamer CALIFORNIA (John Hayes), from Portland via Nanaimo.

19 June   Bktn. CONSTITUTION (J. Robertson), from S.F.

21 June   Steamer GEORGE S. WRIGHT (Nat. L. Rodgers), from Portland.

 7 July   U.S.S.S. SARANAC (James H. Spotts), from a cruise on Puget
          Sound, W.T. Admiral Winslow and family on board
          cruising in the waters of the North Pacific.

22 July   Steamer CALIFORNIA (John Hayes), from Portland, Ore.

29 July   U.S. Revenue Cutter RELIANCE (J.A. Webster, Jr.), from Port
          Townsend, W.T.

 5 Aug.   Schooner PETALUMA (A. Charitonoff), from Kodiak.

14 Aug.   Steamer GEORGE S. WRIGHT (Thomas J. Ainsley), from Portland
          and Port Townsend.

19 Aug.   Schooner SARAH (J.H. Bruce), from S.F.

19 Sept. Steamer GUSSIE TELFAIR (Thomas J. Ainsley), from Portland
          and Nanaimo.

21 Sept. U.S. Revenue Cutter RELIANCE (John A. Webster, Jr.), from
          Kodiak and Ounalaska with Collector Kapus on
          board returned from inspecting tour in Northern
          part of District.

11 Oct.   Schooner SITKA (Henry Theine), from Kutisenoo. Cargo deer
          skins.

14 Oct.   Ship CEZAROWITCH (John A. May), from S.F.

18 Oct.   Schooner PAGE (J. Robertson), from S.F.

21 Oct.   Steamer GEORGE S. WRIGHT (Thomas J. Ainsley), from Portland
          via Nanaimo.

21 Nov.   Steamer GUSSIE TELFAIR (Thomas J. Ainsley), from Portland and
          Nanaimo.

27 May   U.S. Revenue Steamer LINCOLN (Lieut. C.L. Hooper), for Port
         Townsend.

3 June   Steamer CALIFORNIA (John Hayes), for Portland via Nanaimo.

22 June Steamer GEORGE S. WRIGHT (Nat. L. Rogers), for Portland
         via Nanaimo.

17 July U.S.F.S. SARANAC (James H. Spotts), for Port Townsend
         direct.

23 July Steamer CALIFORNIA (John Hayes), for Portland.

28 July Schooner SWEEPSTAKES (William Phillips), for Hamilton
         Fishery.

31 July Barkentine CONSTITUTION (J. Robertson), for S.F.

7 Aug.   U.S. Revenue Cutter RELIANCE (John H. Webster), for cruise
         to Kodiak and Ounalaska.

16 Aug. Barkentine CONSTITUTION, having cleared on the 31st day of
         July did not set sail from the Bay until the
         16th day of August 1871.

16 Aug. Steamer GEORGE S. WRIGHT (Thomas J. Ainsley), for Nanaimo
         and Portland.

17 Aug. Schooner PETALUMA (A. Charitonoff), for Kodiak.

23 Aug. Schooner SARAH (J.H. Bruce), for S.F. via Clawack, A.T.

20 Sept. Steamer GUSSIE TELFAIR (J. Ainsley), for Victoria via
         Kassan and Nanaimo.

29 Sept. Schooner SITKA (Henry Thein), for Kutisenoo, Alaska.

20 Oct. Ship CEZAROWITCH (John A. May), for Kodiak.

23 Oct. Steamer GEORGE S. WRIGHT (Thomas J. Ainsley), for Nanaimo
         and Portland.

31 Oct. Schooner PAGE (J. Robertson), for S.F.

23 Nov. Steamer GUSSIE TELFAIR (Thomas J. Ainsley), for Portland.

27 Dec.   Steamer GUSSIE TELFAIR (Thomas J. Ainsley), from Portland
          and Nanaimo.

<u>1872</u>

12 Jan.   Schooner SWEEPSTAKES (William Phillips), from Clawack.

26 Jan.   Steamer GUSSIE TELFAIR (Thomas J. Ainsley), from Portland
          and Nanaimo.

 6 Feb.   Schooner SITKA (Henry Thein), from trading voyage.

16 Feb.   Steamer GUSSIE TELFAIR (Thomas J. Ainsley), from Portland
          and Nanaimo.

13 Mar.   Steamer GUSSIE TELFAIR (Thomas J. Ainsley), from Portland
          and Nanaimo.

16 Mar.   Schooner PETALUMA (John Kashevarov), from Kodiak.

21 Mar.   U.S. Schooner MARGARET (Comdr. George W. Harris), from
          Lazarus Rock.

26 Mar.   U.S. Schooner MARGARET (George W. Harris), returns from
          cruise.

 3 Apr.   Brig T.W. LUCUS (W.S. Tuttle), from S.F.

 8 Apr.   Schooner URANIA (H. Ravens), from S.F.

11 Apr.   Steamer GUSSIE TELFAIR (Thomas J. Ainsley), from Portland
          and Nanaimo.

12 Apr.   Schooner SITKA (Henry Thein), from trading voyage.

25 Nov.   Schooner SITKA (Henry Thein), for trading voyage in the
          District.

12 Dec.   U.S. Schooner MARGARET (Comodore Harris), for the Alaska
          Hunting Grounds.

28 Dec.   Steamer GUSSIE TELFAIR (Thomas J. Ainsley), for Nanaimo and
          Portland.

<u>1872</u>

24 Jan.   Schooner NELLIE MARTIN (William Stevens), for Fort Tongass.

27 Jan.   Steamer GUSSIE TELFAIR (Thomas J. Ainsley), for Portland
          and Nanaimo.

27 Jan.   Schooner SWEEPSTAKES (William Phillips), for Clowock.

19 Feb.   Steamer GUSSIE TELFAIR (Thomas J. Ainsley), for Portland,
          direct.

23 Feb.   Schooner SITKA (Henry Theine), for trading voyage within
          district.

15 Mar.   Steamer GUSSIE TELFAIR (Thomas J. Ainsley), for Portland,
          direct.

19 Mar.   U.S. Schooner MARGARET (Comdr. George W. Harris), for
              pleasure voyage to the Sulphur Springs.

21 Mar.   Schooner PETALUMA (John Kashevarov), for Kodiak and way
          ports.

22 Mar.   U.S. Schooner MARGARET (Comdr. George W. Harris). Having
              endeavored in vain to beat out of the Harbor,
              now makes the fourth attempt to reach the
              Sulphur Springs.

 9 Apr.   Schooner URANIA (Henry Ravens), for S.F. via trading voyage.

10 Apr.   Brig T.W. LUCUS (W.S. Tuttle), for Port Townsend.

13 Apr.   Steamer GUSSIE TELFAIR (Thomas J. Ainsley), for Portland
          and Nanaimo.

15 Apr.   U.S. Revenue Cutter RELIANCE (Capt. J.A. Webster, Jr.),
              for a cruise to Kodiac and Ounalaska.

Arrivals

 1 May   Schooner SITKA (Henry Theine), from the Hot Springs.

 9 May   Steamer GUSSIE TELFAIR (Thomas J. Ainsley), from Portland.

13 May   Steamer H.M. HUTCHINSON (S.H. Partridge), from S.F.

21 May   U.S. Revenue Cutter RELIANCE (John A. Webster, Jr.), from
          Kodiak and Ounalaska.

22 May   Schooner MARGARET (George W. Harris), from the Sulphur
          Springs.

 6 June Schooner SITKA (Henry Theine), from trading voyage.

11 June Schooner VIVID (George W. Holden), from S.F.

28 June Steamship IDAHO (J.D. Howell), from Portland.

 3 July Steamer ROSE (Allen B. Francis), from Tongass.

11 July Steamer GEORGE S. WRIGHT (Thomas J. Ainsley), from Portland
          and Nanaimo.

 9 Aug. Steamer ROSE (Allen B. Francis), from Cross Sound.

18 Aug. Steamship GEORGE S. WRIGHT (Thomas J. Ainsley), from
          Portland and Nanaimo.

19 Aug. Schooner PAGE (Andrew Live), from S.F.

14 Sept. GEORGE S. WRIGHT (Thomas J. Ainsley), from Portland and
          Nanaimo.

16 Oct. Steamer GEORGE S. WRIGHT (Thomas J. Ainsley), from Port
          Townsend and Nanaimo.

16 Apr. Schooner SITKA (Henry Theine), for the Hot Springs.

10 May   Steamer GUSSIE TELFAIR (Thomas J. Ainsley), for Portland and
         Nanaimo.

11 May   Schooner SITKA (Henry Theine), for a trading voyage.

13 May   Steamer H.M. HUTCHINSON (S.H. Partridge), for Petropolovsky
         and Kodiak.

14 May   Schooner MARGARET (George W. Harris), for a cruise to the
         Hot Springs.

13 June Schooner VIVID (George W. Holden), for Kodiak.

29 June Steamship IDAHO (Jeff D. Howell), for Nanaimo and S.F.

13 July Steamer GEORGE S. WRIGHT (Thomas J. Ainsley), for Nanaimo
         and Portland via way ports.

27 July Steamer ROSE (Allen B. Francis), for Cross Sound.

20 Aug. Steamship GEORGE S. WRIGHT (Thomas J. Ainsley), for
         Portland and Nanaimo.

24 Aug. Schooner PAGE (Andrew Love), for Kodiak.

30 Aug. Steamer ROSE (Allen B. Francis), for Port Townsend and
         Nanaimo.

16 Sept. Steamer GEORGE S. WRIGHT (Thomas J. Ainsley), for Nanaimo
          and Portland.

19 Oct. Steamer GEORGE S. WRIGHT (Thomas J. Ainsley), for Nanaimo
         and Portland.

17 Nov.   Steamer GEORGE S. WRIGHT (Thomas J. Ainsley), from Portland and Nanaimo.

11 Dec.   Steamer GEORGE S. WRIGHT (Thomas J. Ainsley), from Portland.

28 Dec.   Steamer ALEXANDER (M.C. Erskine), from S.F.

<u>1873</u>

19 Jan.   Steamer GEORGE S. WRIGHT (Thomas J. Ainsley), from Portland and Nanaimo.

3 Mar.   Steamer GUSSIE TELFAIR (John Hayes), from Portland and Nanaimo.

17 Apr.   Schooner ANNA MATHILDE (Lewis Merrill), from S.F.

9 May   Schooner NELLIE EDES (William Wastrekoff), from trading voyage.

17 May   Steamer CALIFORNIA (John Hayes), from Port Townsend and Nanaimo.

3 June   Schooner SITKA (Michael Sullivan), from "Hutzenoo".

11 June   Steamer CALIFORNIA (John Hayes), from Port Townsend.

5 July   Steamer CALIFORNIA (John Hayes), from Port Townsend and Nanaimo.

30 Oct.   Schooner SITKA (Michael Sullivan), for Hutsenoo.

19 Nov.   Steamer GEORGE S. WRIGHT (Thomas J. Ainsley), for Portland
          and Nanaimo.

23 Nov.   Schooner ENERGY (George W. Holden), for S.F. via Clawack.

13 Dec.   Steamer GEORGE S. WRIGHT (Thomas J. Ainsley), for Portland.

<u>1873</u>

 4 Jan.   Steamer ALEXANDER (Melvin C. Erskine), for S.F.

21 Jan.   Steamer GEORGE S. WRIGHT (Thomas J. Ainsley), for Portland
          and Nanaimo.
          (Vessel lost, with all on board, about 27 Jan.)

 5 Mar.   Steamer GUSSIE TELFAIR (John Hayes), for Portland and
          Nanaimo.

13 Mar.   Schooner NELLIE EDES (William Wastrekoff), for Clawock.

26 Apr.   Schooner ANNA MATHILDE (Lewis Merrill), for S.F. via Cook
          Inlet.

28 Apr.   Steamer CALIFORNIA (John Hayes), for Portland, direct.

 3 May   Revenue Cutter RELIANCE (John A. Webster, Jr.), for Port
          Townsend.

17 May   Schooner NELLIE EDES (John Panouskoff), for Behrings Bay
          trading.

19 May   Steamer CALIFORNIA (John Hayes), for Nanaimo and Port
          Townsend.

12 June   Schooner SITKA (Michael Sullivan), for Kutsenoo.

13 June   Steamer CALIFORNIA (John Hayes), for Portland.

 6 July   Steamer CALIFORNIA (John Hayes), for Portland direct.

<u>Arrivals</u>

7 July   Schooner NELLIE EDES (John Panousokoff), from trading
voyage.

25 July   Revenue Cutter RELIANCE (Capt. Baker), from Port Townsend.

26 July   Schooner SITKA (Michael Sullivan), from trading voyage.

27 July   Steamer CALIFORNIA (John Hayes), from Portland.

2 Aug.   U.S.S.S. SARANAC (   ), with Admiral Pennock (?), on a
cruise in Alaskan waters, from Port Townsend and
Victoria.

12 Aug.   Steamer ROSE (A.B. Francis), from Victoria.

21 Aug.   Steamer GUSSIE TELFAIR (John Hayes), from Portland and
Victoria.

24 Aug.   Revenue Cutter RELIANCE (Capt. J.G. Baker), from Ounalaska,
having made the round trip from this port in
26 days.

27 Aug.   Schooner NELLIE MARTIN (William S. Stevens), from Tongass.

17 Sept.   Steamer CALIFORNIA (John Hayes), from Portland.

10 Oct.   Schooner NELLIE MARTIN (William J. Stevens), from Clowock.

18 Oct.   Schooner SITKA (Michael Sullivan), from Hootzenoo.

27 Oct.   Steamer CALIFORNIA (John Hayes), from Portland.

26 Nov.   Steamer CALIFORNIA (John Hayes), from Portland, Ore.

28 Nov.   Schooner NELLIE EDES (Evan Panouskoff), from trading voyage.

26 Dec.   Steamer CALIFORNIA (John Hayes), from Portland.

23 July   Schooner SITKA (Michael Sullivan), for trading voyage.

28 July   Steamship CALIFORNIA (John Hayes), for Portland direct.

28 July   Revenue Cutter RELIANCE (Capt. J. G. Baker), for Kodiak and
          Ounalaska.

19 Aug.   U.S.S.S. SARANAC (   ), for S.F. via Port Townsend.

22 Aug.   Steamer GUSSIE TELFAIR (John Hayes), for Nanaimo and
          Portland.

22 Aug.   Sloop ALASKA (George H. Dickinson), for Tongass.

18 Sept. Cutter RELIANCE (J.G. Baker), for Port Townsend.

21 Sept. Schooner SITKA (Michael Sullivan), for Hootzenoo.

22 Sept. Steamer CALIFORNIA (John Hayes), for Portland.

22 Sept. Schooner NELLIE MARTIN (William J. Stevens), for Clowock.

29 Oct.   Steamer CALIFORNIA (John Hayes), for Portland.

 5 Nov.   Schooner NELLIE MARTIN (William J. Stevens), for trading
          voyage.

27 Nov.   Steamer CALIFORNIA (John Hayes), for Portland via Nanaimo.

27 Dec.   Steamer CALIFORNIA (John Hayes), for Portland and Nanaimo.

<u>1874</u>

3 Feb.   Steamer CALIFORNIA (John Hayes), from Portland.

3 Mar.   Steamer CALIFORNIA (John Hayes), from Portland and Nanaimo.

23 Mar.   Steamer ROSE (E.H. Francis), from Port Wrangell. Bearing
             news of loss of U.S. Schooner MARGARET.

27 Mar.   Steamship CALIFORNIA (John Hayes), from Portland via Port
             Townsend.

18 Apr.   Steamship CALIFORNIA (John Hayes), from Portland via
             Victoria and Nanaimo.

2 May   Steam yacht ROSE (E.H. Francis), from Silver Bay.

3 May   U.S.C.S. Schooner YOUKON, from S.F., 13 days.

18 May   Steamship CALIFORNIA (John Hayes), from Portland and Nanaimo.

6 June   Schooner NELLIE EDES (Phillips), from trading voyage, at
             5 o'cl PM.

8 June   Revenue Cutter RELIANCE (Capt. Jno. G. Baker), at 8:30 AM.

10 June   Steamship CALIFORNIA (John Hayes), from Portland and Victoria

29 June   Schooner NELLIE EDES (William Phillips), from trading voyage.

8 July   Schooner BUD (A. Rewrick?), from S.F., "arrived in tow of
             steamer ROSE at 7 PM July 7th, 45 days from San F.,
             15 days off Sitka Harbor."

4 Feb.   Steamship CALIFORNIA (John Hayes), for Portland and Victoria

16 Feb. U.S. Schooner MARGARET (George W. Harris), for San Juan
         Island.
         Wrecked at 2 A.M., 2 March, off north side of
         Kake Islands in heavy snow storm. Total loss.
         All hands saved.

5 Mar.   Steamship CALIFORNIA (John Hayes), for Portland and Nanaimo.

11 Mar. Steamer ROSE (E.H. Francis), for Port Wrangell.

28 Mar. Steamship CALIFORNIA (John Hayes), for Portland via Port
         Townsend.

20 Apr. Steamship CALIFORNIA (John Hayes), for Nanaimo and Portland.
         At 4 o'cl. P.M.

2 May   Steam yacht ROSE (E.H. Francis), for Silver Bay.

11 May   Schooner NELLIE EDES (William Phillips), cleared for trading
         voyage in the "Waters of Alaska."

11 May   U.S.C.S. Schooner YUKON (Warrenden?), for "French Harbor."

12 May   Schooner NELLIE EDES (William Phillips). Sailed at 10:15 AM.

19 May   Steamship CALIFORNIA (John Hayes), for Nanaimo.

8 June   Schooner NELLIE EDES (William Phillipson), cleared for
         trading voyage in the Waters of Alaska, 5 PM.
         Sailed 9 June at 9:45 AM

12 June Revenue Cutter RELIANCE (Jno. G. Baker), for Ounalaska
         (Towed out by ROSE), at 9 AM.

12 June Steamship CALIFORNIA (John Hayes), for Nanaimo and Portland.

8 July   Schooner NELLIE EDES (William Phillips), for trading voyage
         in waters of Alaska. Sailed PM July 9.

Arrivals

11 July Steamship CALIFORNIA (John Hayes), from Portland and
     Victoria, 9 AM. Arrived at wharf 3:30 o'c. AM.

14 Aug. Schooner NELLIE EDES (William Phillips), from trading voyage
10 AM   in waters of Alaska. Arrived at 9 o'c. AM.

17 Aug. Steamship CALIFORNIA (John Hayes), from Portland. Arrived
     at 9 o'c. 16th inst.

14 Sept. Steamship CALIFORNIA (John Hayes), from Portland, Ore. and
     Victoria.

14 Sept. Steamer ROSE (Edwin T. Francis), on trading voyage.

4 Oct. Br. Steamer OTTER (H.G. Lewis), from Victoria via Wrangell,
     visits Sitka for clearance the Depty at that
     Port being under arrest.

5 Oct. Schooner NELLIE EDES (William Phillips), from trading
     voyage, Alaska.

24 Oct. Steamship CALIFORNIA (John Hayes), from Portland and
     Victoria.

10 Nov. Schooner MARIA (George W. Holden), from Kodiac, Alaska.

19 Dec. Steamship GUSSIE TELFAIR (John Hayes), from Portland via
     Nanaimo.

1875

23 Jan. Steamship CALIFORNIA (John Hayes), from Portland and
     Victoria.

22 Feb. Steamship CALIFORNIA (John Hayes), from Portland and
     Victoria.

7 Mar. Steamer ROSE (E.H. Francis), from Hootzenoo and trading
     voyage in waters of Alaska.

11 July   Steamship CALIFORNIA (John Hayes), for Nanaimo and Portland.
          Sailed at 6:20 PM Sunday July 12.

14 July   Schooner BUD (A. Rewrick?), for S.F. via trading voyage in
          waters of Alaska.

18 Aug.   Schooner NELLIE EDES (William Phillips), for Point Baker
          and trading voyage in waters of Alaska.

18 Aug.   Steamship CALIFORNIA (John Hayes), for Nanaimo.

16 Sept. Steamship CALIFORNIA (John Hayes), for Portland via
          Nanaimo.

29 Sept. Steamer ROSE (Edwin T. Francis), from trading voyage.
          (Note: <u>from</u> should probably read <u>for</u>).

 5 Oct.   Br. Steamer OTTER (H.G. Lewis), for Wrangle, Alaska.
          W.B. Daniels on board as acting special Deputy
          Collector at Wrangle.

26 Oct.   Steamship CALIFORNIA (John Hayes), for Portland via Nanaimo.

12 Nov.   Schooner URANIA (George W. Holden), for S.F.

23 Dec.   Steamship GUSSIE TELFAIR (John Hayes), for Portland via
          Nanaimo.

<u>1875</u>

26 Jan.   Steamship CALIFORNIA (John Hayes), for Portland via Nanaimo
          and Victoria.

24 Feb.   Steamship CALIFORNIA (John Hayes), for Portland via Nanaimo
          and Victoria.

 2 Mar.   Steamer ROSE (E.H. Francis), for Hootzenue and trading
          voyage in waters of Alaska.

 3 Mar.   Schooner NELLIE EDES (William Phillips), for trading voyage
          in waters of Alaska.

 9 Mar.   Steamship GUSSIE TELFAIR (John A. Gardner), from Portland
             and Victoria.

22 Mar.   Schooner SITKA (Michael Sullivan), from Wrangle, via
             Hootzenoo.

24 Mar.   Steamship CALIFORNIA (John Hayes), from Portland via
             Victoria.

19 Apr.   Steamship CALIFORNIA (John Hayes), from Portland via
             Victoria.

 4 May   Schooner CALIFORNIA (Edward Howard), from S.F.

10 May   Schooner NELLIE EDES (William Phillips), from Wrangle,
             Tongass, Clawock.

15 May   Steamship CALIFORNIA (John Hayes), from Portland and Victoria.

16 May   Steamer ROSE (Edwin H. Francis), from Stikan and ports in
             Alaska. Brot prisoners, Cutter and Shurick.

 1 June   Schooner NELLIE EDES (William Phillips), from Bearings Bay
             Trading voyage.

10 June   Steamship CALIFORNIA (John Hayes), from Portland and
             Victoria. General Howard and Staff.

19 June   U.S. Revenue Steamer OLIVER WOLCOTT (1st Lieut. Howard),
             from Port Townsend. Centennial Commissioner on
             board.

19 June   Steamer ROSE (Edwin H. Francis), from Hootzenoue, Alaska.
             Capt. Campbell on board.

24 June   Schooner NELLIE EDES (William Phillips), from Chilkat and
             Trading Voyage.

25 June   Schooner CALIFORNIA (Edward Howard), from Kodiac. "Sheean
             on board."

11 July   Steamship CALIFORNIA (John Hayes), from Port Townsend and
             Victoria.

17 July   Schooner NELLIE EDES (William Phillips), from Shagan, Alaska,
             trading voyage.

10 Mar.   Steamship GUSSIE TELFAIR (John A. Gardner), for Nanaimo and
          Portland.

25 Mar.   Steamship CALIFORNIA (John Hayes), for Portland via Nanaimo.

 5 Apr.   Schooner SITKA (Michael Sullivan), for Hootzenoo.

21 Apr.   Steamship CALIFORNIA (John Hayes), for Portland via Nanaimo
          and Victoria.

 5 May   Steamer ROSE (E.H. Francis), for Prince of Wales Island under
          charter to the Commanding Officer of this port.

 7 May   Schooner CALIFORNIA (Edward Howard), for Kodiak.

17 May   Steamship CALIFORNIA (John Hayes), for Victoria via Nanaimo
          and Portland.

19 May   Schooner NELLIE EDES (William Phillips), for Bearings Bay
          on Trading voyage.

 3 June   Schooner NELLIE EDES (William Phillips), for Chilkat on
          Trading voyage.

15 June   Steamship CALIFORNIA (John Hayes), for Chilkat and ports in
          Alaska with Gen. O.O. Howard, thence to Port
          Townsend, W.T.

16 June   Steamer ROSE (E.H. Francis), for Hootzenoo and to meet the
          CALIFORNIA at Cake.

22 June   U.S. Revenue Steamer OLIVER WALCOTT (M.L. Scammon), for
          cruise in the southern waters of Alaska.

25 June   Schooner NELLIE EDES (William Phillips), for Shakan, A.T.
          Gen. Hamilton on Board.

30 June   Schooner CALIFORNIA (Edward Howard), for S.F.

14 July   Steamship CALIFORNIA (John Hayes), for Nanaimo and Port
          Townsend.

27 July   Schooner NELLIE EDES (A.G. Cozian), for Berings Bay and
          Trading Voyage.

20 Aug.   Steamship CALIFORNIA (John Hayes), from Port Townsend and
           Victoria. On board Rev. E.P. Hammond and wife,
           Maj. Boyle, Bachelder and other army officers.

 4 Sept.   Schooner NELLIE EDES (A.G. Cozian), from Bearing's Bay and
           Trading Voyage in waters of Alaska.

17 Sept.   Steamship CALIFORNIA (John Hayes), from Port Townsend and
           Victoria.

15 Oct.   Steamship CALIFORNIA (John Hayes).

15 Oct.   Steamship GUSSIE TELFAIR (J.A. Gardiner), from Port Townsend
           and Victoria.

22 Oct.   Schooner OTSEGO (G.W. Holden), from S.F. via Peterpaulsky,
           R. Poss.

30 Nov.   Steamship CALIFORNIA (John Hayes), from Victoria B.C. and
           Port Townsend.

<u>1876</u>

17 Jan.   Steamship CALIFORNIA (John Hayes), from Victoria and Port
           Townsend.

 1 Feb.   Bark WILLIAM H. THORNDIKE (D.D. Kelly, Jr.), from Philadel-
           phia, Pa., loaded with Naval coal.

20 Feb.   Steamship CALIFORNIA (John Hayes), from Port Townsend and
           Victoria.

18 Mar.   Steamship CALIFORNIA (John Hayes), from Port Townsend and
           Victoria.

17 Apr.   Steamship CALIFORNIA (John Hayes), from Port Townsend and
           Victoria.

 6 May   Schooner NELLIE EDES (George Cozian), from Klawack, A.T.

11 May   Steamer CALIFORNIA (John Hayes), from Port Townsend via
           Nanaimo.

14 June   Steamship CALIFORNIA (John Hayes), from Port Townsend and
           Nanaimo. Col. Mendenhall and three companies
           on board.

17 July   Steamship CALIFORNIA (J.A. Gardiner), from Port Townsend and
           Nanaimo. 2:30 PM.

21 July   Schooner NELLIE EDES (A.G. Cozian), from Newchuck R. and
           Trading voyage. Midnight.

22 Aug.   Steamship CALIFORNIA (John Hayes), for Victoria and Port
          Townsend.

20 Sept. Steamship CALIFORNIA (John Hayes), for Victoria via
          Nanaimo.

ca. 16 Oct.   Steamship CALIFORNIA.

18 Oct.   Steamship GUSSIE TELFAIR (J.A. Gardiner), for Victoria via
          Nanaimo and Portland.

28 Oct.   Schooner OTSEGO (G.W. Holden), for S.F.

 6 Dec.   Steamship CALIFORNIA (John Hayes), for Victoria via Nanaimo.

<u>1876</u>

20 Jan.   Steamship CALIFORNIA (John Hayes), for Victoria and Port
          Townsend. Maj. Berry on board.

22 Feb.   Steamship CALIFORNIA (John Hayes), for Victoria and Port
          Townsend.

11 Mar.   Bark WILLIAM H. THORNDIKE (D.D. Kelly, Jr.), for Astoria,
          Oregon. E.G. Harvey, C.C. Slykes and wife on
          board.

20 Mar.   Steamship CALIFORNIA (John Hayes), for Victoria.

19 Apr.   Steamship CALIFORNIA (John Hayes), for Victoria.

16 May   Schooner NELLIE EDES (George Cozian), for Bristol Bay and
          trading voyage.

17 June   Steamship CALIFORNIA (John Hayes), for Port Townsend and
          Nanaimo. On board Campbell and command.

19 July   Steamship CALIFORNIA (J.A. Gardiner), for Port Townsend and
          Victoria via Nanaimo. 3 A.M.

24 July   Schooner OCEAN SPRAY (Thomas Butler), from Ounalaska,
                    Lee Roy Woods, Depty Coll. in charge having
                    seized the same.

29 July   Steamer ROSE (E.H. Francis), from trading voyage Hoona.

23 Aug.   Steamer CALIFORNIA (A. Gardiner), from Port Townsend and
                    Victoria.

22 Sept. Steamship GUSSIE TELFAIR (J.A. Gardiner), from Victoria
                    and Port Townsend.

30 Oct.   Steamship GUSSIE TELFAIR (J.A. Gardiner), from Port
                    Townsend and Victoria.

 8 Dec.   Steamship GUSSIE TELFAIR (J.A. Gardiner), from Port
                    Townsend and Victoria, B.C.

<u>1877</u>

 9 Jan.   Steamship GUSSIE TELFAIR (J.A. Gardiner), from Port
                    Townsend and Victoria.

 9 Feb.   Steamship GUSSIE TELFAIR (J.A. Gardiner), from Port
                    Townsend and Victoria.

 4 Mar.   Steamship CALIFORNIA (Charles Thorne), from Port Townsend
                    and Victoria.

29 Mar.   Steamship CALIFORNIA (Charles Thorne), from Port Townsend
                    and Victoria. Inspector Mason on board

11 Apr.   Schooner NELLIE EDES (William Phillips), for trading voyage
                    in waters of Alaska.

15 Apr.   Steamer CALIFORNIA (Charles Thorne), from Port Townsend and
                    Victoria.

 1 May   Schooner SAN DIEGO (R. Bishop), from S.F.

11 May   Steamer CALIFORNIA (Charles Thorne), from Port Townsend and
                    Victoria.

19 May   U.S. Revenue Cutter RICHARD RUSH (G.W. Bailey), from S.F.

11 June   Steamer CALIFORNIA (Charles Thorne), from Port Townsend and
                    Victoria.

12 July   Steamer CALIFORNIA (Charles Thorne), from Port Townsend and
                    Victoria.

25 July   Steamer ROSE (E.H. Francis), for Hoona and trading voyage.

31 July   Schooner OCEAN SPRAY, in charge of Dep. Coll. Lee Roy Woods. Ordered to Portland for trial.

25 Aug.   Steamer CALIFORNIA (J.A. Gardiner), for Port Townsend and Victoria.

24 Sept. Steamship GUSSIE TELFAIR (J.A. Gardiner), for Port Townsend and Victoria.

5 Nov.   Steamship GUSSIE TELFAIR (J.A. Gardiner), for Port Townsend and Victoria.

11 Nov.   Steamship GUSSIE TELFAIR (J.A. Gardiner), for Port Townsend and Victoria.

<u>1877</u>

11 Jan.   Steamship GUSSIE TELFAIR (J.A. Gardiner), for Port Townsend and Victoria.

12 Feb.   Steamship GUSSIE TELFAIR (J.A. Gardiner), for Port Townsend and Nanaimo and Victoria.

5 Mar.   Steamship CALIFORNIA (Charles Thorne), for Port Townsend and Victoria.

30 Mar.   Steamship CALIFORNIA (Charles Thorne), for Port Townsend and Nanaimo.

14 Apr.   Schooner NELLIE MARTIN (James Healy), from (for?) Klawock.

17 Apr.   Steamer CALIFORNIA (Charles Thorne), for Port Townsend and Nanaimo.

11 May   Schooner SAN DIEGO (R. Bishop), for trading, hunting and fishing voyage.

17 May   Steamer CALIFORNIA (Charles Thorne), for Port Townsend and Nanaimo.

21 May   U.S. Revenue Cutter RICHARD RUSH (G.W. Bailey), for Kodiac and Western waters of Alaska.

14 June   Steamer CALIFORNIA (Charles Thorne), for Port Townsend. On board Co. G and M, 4th Arty., Capt. A. Morris, commanding. The Military withdrawn from the Territory of Alaska.

14 July   Steamer CALIFORNIA (Charles Thorne), for Victoria and Port Townsend.

21 July   Schooner NELLIE EDES (William Phillips), from trading
            voyage.

10 Aug.   U.S. Revenue Cutter THOMAS CORWIN (Capt. White), from S.F.
            (Ordered to Sitka at request of Major Berry,
            Collector of Customs, and William Gouverneur
            Morris, special agent of the Treasury Depart-
            ment, to maintain order after departure of the
            military).

11 Aug.   Steamer CALIFORNIA (Charles Thorne), from Port Townsend and
            Victoria.

27 Aug.   U.S. Revenue Cutter THOMAS CORWIN (Capt. White), from
            cruise in Alaska waters.

14 Sept. U.S. Mail Steamer CALIFORNIA (Charles Thorne), from Port
            Townsend and Victoria.

16 Oct.   U.S. Revenue Cutter OLIVER WOLCOTT (Capt. J.M. Selden),
            from Port Townsend.

21 Oct.   U.S. Mail Steamer CALIFORNIA (Charles Thorne), from Port
            Townsend and Victoria.

14 Nov.   Steamship CALIFORNIA (Charles Thorne), from Port Townsend
            and Victoria.

 2 Dec.   Sloop GOLD HUNTER (James Holywood), from trading cruise.

16 Dec.   Steamer CALIFORNIA (Charles Thorne), from Port Townsend and
            Victoria.

<u>1878</u>

14 Jan.   Steamship CALIFORNIA (Charles Thorne), from Port Townsend
            and Victoria.

19 Feb.   Steamship CALIFORNIA (Charles Thorne), from Port Townsend
            and Victoria.

16 Mar.   Steamship CALIFORNIA (Charles Thorne), from Port Townsend
            and Victoria.

11 Apr.   Steamship CALIFORNIA (Charles Thorne), from Port Townsend
            and Victoria.

 1 May   U.S. Revenue Cutter OLIVER WOLCOTT (J.M. Selden), from Port
            Townsend.

13 Aug.   Steamer CALIFORNIA (Charles Thorne), for Victoria via Nanaimo and Port Townsend.

20 Aug.   U.S. Revenue Cutter THOMAS CORWIN (Capt. White), for cruise in Alaska waters.

28 Aug.   U.S. Revenue Cutter THOMAS CORWIN (Capt. White), for Puget Sound via several points in Alaska.

15 Sept.   U.S. Mail Steamer CALIFORNIA (Charles Thorne), for Port Townsend and Victoria.

22 Oct.   U.S. Mail Steamer CALIFORNIA (Charles Thorne), for Port Townsend and Victoria.

2 Nov.   U.S. Revenue Cutter OLIVER WOLCOTT (J.M. Selden), for Port Townsend and Victoria, B.C.

16 Nov.   Steamship CALIFORNIA (Charles Thorne), for Port Townsend and Victoria.

17 Dec.   Steamer CALIFORNIA (Charles Thorne), to Port Townsend and Victoria.

<u>1878</u>

15 Jan.   Steamship CALIFORNIA (Charles Thorne), for Victoria and Port Townsend.

20 Feb.   Steamship CALIFORNIA (Charles Thorne), for Victoria and Port Townsend.

17 Mar.   Steamship CALIFORNIA (Charles Thorne), for Victoria and Port Townsend.

12 Apr.   Steamship CALIFORNIA (Charles Thorne), for Victoria and Port Townsend.

14 May   Steamship CALIFORNIA (Charles Thorne), from Port Townsend
              and Victoria.

3 June   Steamship ROSE (William Phillips), from Chilcat, Alaska.

13 June Steamship CALIFORNIA (Charles Thorne), from Port Townsend
              via Victoria.

8 July   Steamer CALIFORNIA (Charles Thorne), from Port Townsend
              via Victoria.

8 July   Steamer ROSE (Philip Kashevaroff), from cruise within the
              District.

7 May   U.S. Revenue Cutter OLIVER WOLCOTT (J.M. Selden), for Port
        Townsend via Wrangel, A.T.

15 May Steamship CALIFORNIA (Charles Thorne), for Victoria and
        Port Townsend.

27 May Steamer ROSE (William Phillips), for Chilcat, Alaska.

15 June Steamship CALIFORNIA (Charles Thorn), for Victoria and
         Port Townsend.

19 June Steamer ROSE (Phillip Kashevaroff), for cruise within
         District.

10 July Steamer CALIFORNIA (Charles Thorne), for Victoria and
         Port Townsend.

MASTERS AND VESSELS AT SITKA, 1867-1878

(Dates indicate appearance in foregoing list).

Ainsley, Thomas J. Steamer GUSSIE TELFAIR, 1871.

Bailey, George W. U.S.R.C. RICHARD RUSH, 1877. Lost overboard,
     15 October 1879.

Baker, J.G., Capt. U.S.R.C. RELIANCE, 1873.

Baronovich (or Baranowicz), Vincent. Schooner PIONEER, 1870.

Bendel, B. Schooner NOR'WESTER, 1868.

Benzemann. Steamer CONSTANTINE, 1868; Russian ship WINGED ARROW,
     1868.

Bishop, R. Schooner SAN DIEGO, 1877.

Boucht. Bark Cyane, 1867.

Bruce, J.H. Schooner SARAH, 1871.

Butler, Thomas. Schooner OCEAN SPRAY, 1876.

Charitonoff, A. Schooner PETALUMA, 1871.

Coffin, Horace ("Tom"). Schooner GROWLER, 1867, 1868. Lost, with
     vessel, after leaving Victoria on 19 March 1868, for Sitka.

Comstock. Bark PERU, 1868.

Cook, John. Steamer MAJOR, 1869; schooner NOR'WESTER, 1870.

Cooper. H.M.S. SPARROWHAWK, 1867.

Cozian, A.G. (Anton George?). Schooner LANGLEY, 1868; schooner
     NELLIE EDES, 1875.

Dall, C.C. ("Chris"). Steamer JOHN L. STEPHENS, 1867; steamer
     ACTIVE, 1869.

Den'gin, George. Russian brig SHELEKHOV, 1867.

Dickinson, George. Schooner SWEEPSTAKES, 1871; sloop ALASKA, 1873.

Doyle, Edward. Schooner EDWIN H. FRANCIS, 1870.

Erskine, Melville C. Steamer FIDELITER, 1867, 1868; steamer
     ALEXANDER, 1868, 1872; steamer CONSTANTINE, 1869.

Eusalius. Russian ship TSARITSA, 1867.

Evans, David. U.S.R.C. LINCOLN, 1869.

Ferguson. Schooner BLACK DIAMOND, 1868.

Francis, Allen B. Steamer ROSE, 1872.

Francis, Edwin H. Steamer ROSE, 1875, 1876.

Freeman, William Jr. U.S. Transport NEWBERN, 1869.

Gardner, John A. Steamer GUSSIE TELFAIR, 1874, 1875.

Hanson, John. Brig CONSTANTINE, 1867.

Harris, George W. Schooner MARGARET, 1870, 1871.

Hayes, John. Steamer CALIFORNIA, 1871; steamer GUSSIE TELFAIR, 1872.

Healy, James. Schooner NELLIE MARTIN, 1877.

Heiffer, A. Schooner SWEEPSTAKES, 1868.

Henriques, Capt. J.A. U.S.R.C. LINCOLN, 1869.

Hewitt, J.H. Schooner PETALUMA, 1870.

Holcomb, N. Schooner CALDERA, 1868; schooner PAGE, 1869.

Holden, George W. Schooner VIVID, 1872; schooner ENERGY, 1872;
    schooner MARIA, 1874; schooner URANIA, 1874; schooner OTSEGO,
    1875.

Holmes, Peter. British steamer EMMA, 1868, 1869.

Holtern (Haltern?). Schooner SWEEPSTAKES, 1868.

Holywood, James. Sloop GOLD HUNTER, 1878.

Hooper, C.L., Lieut. U.S.R.C. LINCOLN, 1871.

Hopkins, Alfred. U.S. Ship CYANE, 1870.

Howard. U.S.R.C. LINCOLN, 1867.

Howard, Edward. Schooner CALIFORNIA, 1875.

Howell, Jeff D. Steamship IDAHO, 1872.

Ignatieff, Makar. Schooner EDWIN H. FRANCIS, 1870.

Ivanoff, Thicken (?). Schooner CLARA L. WEST, 1871.

Kashevaroff (Kashevarov). Bark MENSHIKOFF, 1868; schooner PIONEER,
    1868; schooner PETALUMA, 1872.

Kashevaroff, Phillip. Steamer ROSE, 1878.

Keene, James W. Schooner SWEEPSTAKES, 1869.

Kelly, Jr., D.D. Bark WILLIAM H. THORNDIKE, 1875.

Kelton, A.K. Bark BUENAVISTA, 1868.

Killman, Robert. Bark ROBERT PORTER, 1869.

King. U.S. Ship JAMESTOWN, 1867.

Langdon, W. Steamer GEORGE S. WRIGHT, 1868.

Lee, Thomas K. Schooner GENERAL HARNEY, 1869, 1870.

Lewis, Herbert G. British steamer OTTER, 1868, ff.

Lindfors, A. Ship CESAREWITCH, 1867; steamer CONSTANTINE, 1868;
     steamer ALEXANDER, 1868.

Lindstrom, Magnus. Schooner GENERAL HARNEY, 1869.

Live, Andrew. Schooner PAGE, 1869.

Lund, William. Sandwich Island bark MAMELUKE, 1867.

Mason, W.E. Steamer ALEXANDER, 1868; steamer CALIFORNIA, 1868.

May, John A. Ship CEZAROWICH, 1871.

McCulloch, W.C. British schooner BLACK DIAMOND, 1868.

McKay. British schooner ALERT, 1867, 1868.

Merrill, Lewis. ANNA MATHILDE, 1872.

Metcalf, Alfred. Schooner CALIFORNIA, 1870.

Mills, James. Brig L.P. FOSTER, 1870.

Milowanski, John. Schooner LANGLEY, 1867.

Mitchell. Steamer SAGINAW, 1868.

Morgan, Ebenezer. Bark PERU, 1868.

Morrison, J.B. Schooner ANN ELIZA, 1868.

Niebaum, Gustave. Brig CONSTANTINE, 1867; steamer ALEXANDER, 1867.

Partridge, S.H. Steamer H.M. HUTCHINSON, 1872.

Phillips, William P. Schooner NOR'WESTER, 1869, 1870; SWEEPSTAKES,
     1870.

Panouskoff, John. Schooner NELLIE EDES, 1873.

Piggott, Lieut. William C. U.S.R.C. RELIANCE, 1871.

Ravens, Henry. Schooner LOUISA C. SIMPSON, 1870; schooner URANIA,
     1872. Notorious contrabandist, longtime master of schooner
     TIMANDRA. In 1879, lost with schooner ELLEN J. McKINNON.

Rewrick, A. Schooner BUD, 1874.

Rink. Schooner JOHN BRIGHT, 1868.

Robertson. Bark DELAWARE, 1868.

Robertson, J. Barkentine CONSTITUTION, 1871; schooner PAGE, 1871.

Rogers, Nat. L. Steamer CALIFORNIA, 1870; steamer GEORGE S. WRIGHT,
     1870.

Sadler, W.S. Schooner FLYING MIST, 1870.

Sandman, John G. Brig OLGA, 1868, 1870.

Sands, John R. Schooner LEWIS PERRY, 1869; bark CYANE, 1869; ship
     WINGED ARROW, 1868.

Scammon, M.L. U.S.R.C. OLIVER WOLCOTT, 1875.

Schmidberg, A. Ship TSESAREVICH, 1867.

Selden, Capt. James W. U.S.R.C. RELIANCE, 1869, 1870; U.S.R.C.
     OLIVER WOLCOTT, 1877.

Shillaber. Bark DELAWARE, 1867, 1868.

Simpson, J.P. Schooner SHOOTING STAR, 1870.

Slocum, Joshua. Bark CONSTITUTION, 1870.

Small, D.K. Steamer CONSTANTINE, 1870.

Smith, William H. Sloop OCEAN QUEEN, 1868.

Snow. Bark MILAN, 1867.

Spotts, James H. U.S.S. Ship SARANAC, 1870.

Stevens, William. Schooner NELLIE MARTIN, 1871, 1873.

Strachan, James. Schooner MAJOR, 1870.

Sullivan, Michael. Schooner SITKA, 1872, 1873; schooner LOUISA
     DOWNES, 1868; schooner LANGLEY, 1869.

Thein, Henry. Schooner MAJOR, 1869; schooner SITKA, 1871.

Thorne. Charles, Steamship CALIFORNIA, 1877, 1878.

Tuttle, W.S. Brig T.W. LUCAS, 1872.

Waitt, F.C. Steamer GEORGE S. WRIGHT, 1870.

Walker, David. Ship TSESAREWITSCH, 1868.

Walker, James. Schooner MAJOR, 1870.

Walker, John. Schooner MARY TAYLOR, 1870, 1871.

Wardnden. Schooner FLYING MIST, 1870.

Wastrikoff, William. Schooner NELLIE EDES, 1873.

Webster, Jr., John A. U.S.R.C. RELIANCE, 1871, 1873.

White, John W., Capt. U.S.R.C. WAYANDA, 1868; steamer FIDELITER,
     1869; U.S.R.C. THOMAS CORWIN, 1877.

Whitford, A.T. Schooner NOR'WESTER, 1868.

Winsor. Steamer FIDELITER, 1868; steamer PACIFIC, 1868.

ACTIVE, steamer (510.43 tons), 1869.

ALASKA, schooner, 1869.

ALASKA, sloop, 1873.

ALERT, British schooner (30.17 tons), 1868.

ALEXANDER, steamer (500 tons), 1867 ff. Built in New York in 1855,
    rounded Cape Horn with name of ASTORIA, turned over to Russians
    and renamed IMPERATOR ALEKSANDR II. A staunch, fast steamer,
    used for many purposes.

ALICE, schooner, 1869.

ANN ELIZA, schooner, 1868.

ANNA MATHILDE, schooner (34.47 tons), 1872.

BARANOV, steamer. See steamer ROSE.

BLACK DIAMOND, British schooner (63.04 tons), 1868.

BUD, schooner, 1874.

BUENAVISTA, ship (736.56 tons), 1867, 1868.

CALDERA, schooner (83.63 tons), 1868.

CALIFORNIA, steamer (673 tons), 1870, 1871, ff. Earlier known as the
    LITTLE CALIFORNIA, and later as the EUREKA.

CLARA L. WEST, schooner, 1870, 1871.

COMMODORE, brig, 1869.

CONSTANTINE, brig (122.53 tons), 1867.

CONSTANTINE, steamer (319.67 tons), 1868 ff. Operated by Hutchinson,
    Kohl & Co. in 1868. In 1869, sunk three miles south of Active
    Pass; raised and towed to Port Ludlow by steamer FIDELITER.
    Repaired in S.F., resumed in Sitka trade as mail boat. 1871, in
    Portland and S.F. traffic; later on run between Santa Barbara
    and S.F. 1887, broken up.

CONSTITUTION, bark, 1870, 1871.

CYANE, bark, 1867, 1868, 1869.

CYANE, U.S. sloop-of-war, 1869, 1870. Changed from a man of war to
    a store ship at Mare Island in 1856, then sent to Panama, where
    she lay for some time before returning to San Francisco and
    thence to Sitka in summer of 1869. Lay there until December
    1870, when went to Tehuantepec, Mexico.

DELAWARE, bark, 1867, 1868.

60

EDWIN H. FRANCIS, schooner, 1870.

EMMA, British steamer (25.24 tons), 1868, 1869. Built at Victoria.
     Ran until 1891, when a total loss.

ENERGY, schooner, 1872.

FAVORITE, British schooner, 1869. Built in 1869 at Sooke. Later a
     sealer. Seized by U.S. authorities in 1894.

FIDELITER, steamer (175.16 tons), 1867 ff. British built, 1863; much
     used on Northwest Coast. Sank after collision, 1865; repaired
     and resumed in passenger service. By fictitious sale to a
     Russian at Sitka in 1867, owner William Kohl was able to acquire
     U.S. registry in October of that year, after transfer of the
     territory. Wrecked on California coast in October, 1876.

FLYING MIST, schooner, 1870.

FRANCIS PALMER, bark, 1869.

FRANCIS A. STEELE, schooner (79.52 tons), 1868, 1869.

GENERAL HARNEY, schooner, 1868, 1869, 1870. In 1889, wrecked on
     Goose Island in San Juan Passage.

GEORGE S. WRIGHT, steamer (214 tons), 1868, 1869, 1870. Launched at
     Port Ludlow, 1863. In Siberia for Russian-American Telegraph
     Company, 1866-1868. Carried mail to Alaska. Lost, with all on
     board, in 1873.

GOLD HUNTER, sloop, 1877.

GROWLER, schooner (48.50 tons), 1867, 1868. Sailed from Victoria
     on 19 March 1868, for Sitka, and lost off Cape Murray, Queen
     Charlotte Island. All survivors slain by Haida Indians.

GUSSIE TELFAIR, steamer (413.06 tons), 1871, 1872. Built at Greenock
     in 1863 as blockade runner. Captured, sold in New York.
     Wrecked on Coos Bay route, near Marshfield, in 1880.

H.M. HUTCHINSON, steamer (97.08 tons), 1872. Former Revenue Service
     cutter, HARRIET LANE. Purchased by J. Boscowitz in 1869.

IDAHO, schooner, 1869.

IDAHO, steamship (1077.13 tons), 1872. Wrecked in Straits of Fuca,
     29 November 1889.

JABEZ HOWE, sloop, 1868.

JAMESTOWN, U.S. ship, 1867, 1868.

JOHN BRIGHT, schooner, 1868.

JOHN L. STEPHENS, ship, 1867. Built in New York, 1852. Sidewheeler
     with beam engine. Length 275 feet; tonnage 1,836. Sold for use
     as floating cannery in 1878.

KUTUSOFF, bark, 1869.

LANGLEY, schooner (16 tons), 1867, 1868.

LEGAL TENDER, schooner, 1869.

LEWIS PERRY, schooner, 1869.

L.P. FOSTER, brig, 1870.

LINCOLN, U.S. Revenue Cutter, 1867, 1869, 1871. Built in Baltimore,
    brought to Pacific Coast by Capt. J.W. White in 1866. 640 tons,
    screw steamer, crew of 57, armed with 7-inch gun.

LIZZIE SHA, schooner, 1869.

LOUISA C. SIMPSON, schooner, 1870.

LOUISA DOWNES, schooner, 1867, 1868. Wrecked, 1869.

LUELLA, schooner, 1869. Driven ashore on the Alaska coast during a
    gale, in May, 1869. Total loss. Owned by Costello and Malowinski,
    of Victoria.

MAJOR, steamer (5.15 tons), 1869.

MAMELUKE, Sandwich Island bark (750.50 tons), 1867.

MARGARET, U.S. schooner, 1870, 1871. Driven ashore on Alaska coast
    in March, 1874.

MARY TAYLOR, schooner, 1870.

MENSHIKOV, ship, 1867. Russian vessel, sold after sale of Alaska.

MILAN, bark (739 tons), 1867, 1868.

MONTICELLO, bark, 1869.

MYSTERY, schooner, 1867.

NELLIE EDES, schooner, 1874, 1875.

NELLIE MARTIN, schooner (220.50 tons), 1871, 1873.

NEWBERN, U.S. transport, 1869, 1870. Built in Brooklyn in 1862 as the
    United States; purchased by Navy Department and renamed, then
    turned over to Quartermaster Department of Army. Wrecked off
    San Pedro, California, in 1894.

NOR'WESTER, schooner (37.02 tons), 1867, 1868, 1869.

OCEAN SPRAY, schooner, 1876. Seized in Alaska in 1876 on a charge of
    selling liquor to the Indians. Towed to Portland and sold at
    auction.

OCEAN QUEEN, British sloop, 1868.

OLGA, brig, 1868, 1869, 1870.

OTTER, British (Hudson's Bay Company) steamer, 1867 ff. Built in
    England in 1852, about 220 tons. Sank near Bella Coola in 1880;
    raised. Finally used as a coal hulk until June, 1890, when
    burned for copper.

OSSIPEE, U.S. sloop-of-war, 1867.

OTSEGO, schooner, 1875.

PACIFIC, steamship (875.99 tons), 1868. Sidewheeler, built in New
    York in 1851. Lost after collision, 4 November 1875; only two
    survivors out of over 250 crew and passengers.

PAGE, schooner,(109.68 tons), 1869.

PERU, bark, 1868.

PETALUMA, schooner (20.21 tons), 1870, 1871, 1872.

PIONEER, schooner (25 tons), 1868, 1870.

POLITKOFSKY, steamer, 1867. Built at Sitka in 1856 of hewn Alaska
    cedar. Purchased by Hutchinson, Kohl & Co. In use until
    20th century.

RELIANCE, U.S. Revenue Cutter, 1869, 1870, 1871.

RESACA, U.S. war steamer, 1867.

ROBERT PORTER, bark, 1869, 1870.

ROSE, steamer (43.85 tons), 1872, 1878. Built at Sitka in 1862 as
    BARANOV. Purchased by Allen Francis, British consul at Victoria
    in 1871; remodelled, sidewheels removed, fitted with propellor,
    and renamed. In Alaska fur trade until 1873, transferred to
    Island route on Puget Sound, carrying mail. In Fall of 1873,
    returned to Alaska and entered trading business; continued with
    Alaska Oil & Guano Company for many years.

SAGINAW, U.S. steamer, 1868, 1869.

SAN DIEGO, schooner, 1877.

SARANAC, U.S.S. ship, 1870, 1871, 1873.

SARAH, schooner,(105.03 tons), 1871.

SHELIKHOV, brig (213.45 tons), 1869. About September, 1872, lost in
    cyclone enroute from San Francisco to Callao. Only the captain
    survived.

SHOOTING STAR, schooner, 1870.

SITKA, schooner (9.85 tons), 1871.

SPARROWHAWK, H.M.S., 1867. After being stationed at Esquimault for
    several years, purchased by a Portland firm in 1872 and turned
    into a sailing vessel.

SWEEPSTAKES, schooner (23.80 tons), 1868 ff.

T.W. LUCAS, brig (306.78 tons), 1872. Lost off Port Orford, 24 Octo-
    ber 1894.

THOMAS CORWIN, U.S. Revenue cutter, 1877.

THOMAS WOODWARD, schooner (108.90 tons), 1868. On 26 November 1868,
    struck reef at Shelter Point near Cape Mudge. Total loss;
    passengers and mail saved.

THORNTON, British sloop (45 tons), 1868.

TSARITSA, Russian ship (946 tons), 1867. Built in U.S. in 1854.

TSESAREVICH (also CESAREWITCH), ship (294 tons), 1867, 1869, 1871.

URANIA, schooner (80.26 tons), 1871. Under Thomas K. Lee, disappear-
    ed after leaving Kodiak 29 December 1876, with cargo of furs for
    S.F.

VIVID, schooner, 1872.

WILLIAM H. THORNDIKE, bark, 1875.

WAYANDA, U.S. Revenue cutter, 1868, 1869. Renamed LOS ANGELES;
    wrecked at Point Sur, California, 21 April 1894.

WINGED ARROW, American (later Russian) ship (933 tons), 1868.

YOUKON, U.S. Customs Service steamer, 1869, 1874.